Fly Fishing the Colorado River

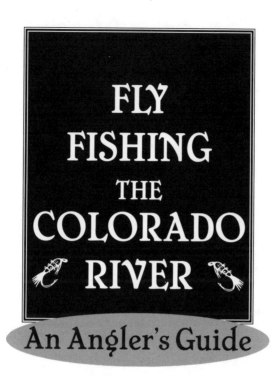

FLY
FISHING
THE
COLORADO
RIVER

An Angler's Guide

Al Marlowe

PRUETT

PRUETT PUBLISHING COMPANY
BOULDER, COLORADO

Printed in the United States
10 9 8 7 6 5 4 3 2 1

Library of Congress Cataloging-in-Publication data

Marlowe, Al, 1938–
    Fly fishing the Colorado River : an angler's guide / Al Marlowe.
        p.   cm.
    Includes bibliographical references (p. 159) and index.
    ISBN 0-87108-885-1 (pbk.)
        1. Fly fishing—Colorado River (Colo.-Mexico)—Guidebooks.
    I. Title.
    SH464.C65M37   1997
    799.1'24'097913—dc21   97-9294
                                                                     CIP

Cover and book design by Kathleen McAffrey, Starr Design
Book composition by Lyn Chaffee
Cover photograph by Al Marlowe

To Skipper,
the Golden Retriever who owns me.
He thinks home is where we stay when we're not fishing.

CONTENTS

ACKNOWLEDGMENTS

Truth is often discovered not by searching but by being stumbled over. I found that the Colorado River is truly a pleasure to visit and fish in just that way. My rediscovery of the river occurred after a long hiatus. As is often the case in other areas of life, sometimes the second time around is better. That was certainly true of the Colorado and me.

I first fished the Colorado in the late sixties. At that time the river had no special angling restrictions—any method was legal. The limit was ten fish per day. Fly fishing wasn't the "in" sport it is now. The river was less crowded. Of course, the fishing was better too. The fishing was always better twenty or thirty years ago. And twenty or thirty years ago, anglers said the same thing.

But today in Middle Park, an angler will find pleasure not only in taking a beautifully marked rainbow or brown but in the wider experience. One might observe a *Baetis* drifting in the current, and rather than immediately changing flies to match the hatch, might marvel at the beauty of the insect as it rides the water: translucent lightly veined wings upright, body outstretched on six legs, ready to fulfill its purpose in its short life. A mule deer emerging through the willows to sip from the river will make the angler forget his reason for being on the stream. The honking of a flight of geese will draw his eyes to the air to watch as they set their wings to alight gently on the river downstream. The angler comes to realize that fly fishing is merely an excuse to observe these other natural events.

Although an author usually takes credit for a book, it's rare that only one person contributes to its production. And even though I readily admit to having brought this work to its present form with some assistance from the publisher and editors, several fellow fly fishermen of both genders also assisted me. The first is Harry Ledyard. Harry is the one who encouraged me to go ahead with my book idea on a warm July day in 1994. That day on the river produced few fish for either of us, but he too saw the potential of the Colorado on his first visit. That the fish didn't cooperate was our problem; neither of us had wanted to arise sufficiently early to get on the water at the proper hour.

Harry also earned my gratitude for responding to my multiple requests to borrow his copy of *Rod and Line in Colorado Waters*, which I perused many times while compiling this book. The more I scan this delightful work from a century ago, the more I realize that its author knew what I know: It's not so much the taking of a few fish that brings rewards but rather the entire angling experience. It's an appreciation for the ancillary encounters that add to the enjoyment of fly fishing.

There's also John Murphy. He's the one who first shared the upper Colorado with me. When I informed him of this book project, John enthusiastically shared his knowledge of the river and his data files. He also assisted with editing early drafts of the manuscript. I appreciate his friendship as well as the valuable suggestions he contributed.

Ken Rupkalvis is responsible for my rediscovery of the Colorado. "I'd really like to get back into fly fishing," Ken told me as we dined in a Denver Holiday Inn restaurant. That was a few years ago, on the day we got acquainted as a result of a common interest in shooting muzzleloaders. I told Ken that as soon as some of the more suitable beginner waters opened up, we'd go wet a line.

At the time in the army band at Fort Carson, Ken's time off either was planned long in advance or was taken on the spur of the moment. A few weeks later he informed me he had leave coming at the end of April and asked if I wanted to take him fly fishing then. Though late April wasn't what I considered the best time to learn fly fishing, I told him I'd find a place that would work. Where could we go, I wondered? There's always Cheesman Canyon on the South Platte, but that's hardly a place for first-time anglers. I didn't enjoy the usual crowds there anyway. High-country beaver ponds or lakes would be ideal but wouldn't open for another two or three months. What about the Fryingpan? It's open all year, but I didn't think it would work either. The Colorado near Hot Sulphur Springs was the only place I could think of that had what we wanted. For camping we needed a place with not too much elevation, so that the snow would be gone. And it should be close by, for we only had three days. The potential for catching fish was necessary, and that meant the Colorado River. Ken and I solidified our plans. We would head for the Colorado and camp beside the river in the Colorado Department of Wildlife's (CDOW) Beaver Creek Unit.

That three-day excursion showed me I had missed out on a grand river adventure during my time away from the Colorado. From our camp at the west end of Byers Canyon we found spawning rainbows. In that three days I caught a few fish, and Ken caught none. We learned that the Colorado has more water in the Middle Park stretch than we could fish in three days. We did try, though, to explore every public access. Maybe that's why we found it easy to fall asleep each night.

Jean, also known as Mrs. Marlowe, helped with this book too. Not only has she tolerated my compulsive angling, but she has accompanied me many times over the years to search for trout in near and faraway places. On an August Sunday in 1994 she accompanied me to the river so I could photograph her catching trout. Jean gave me plenty of opportunities to do the job. She caught a fish so large that the photo of it weighed three pounds, obviously of such size as to preclude inclusion in this book. Maps are necessary if one is to successfully navigate to locations described in this guide. A special thanks goes to my neighbor and fellow outdoorsman Tom Finneran for his assistance in producing the maps and hatch charts reproduced here. We spent several hours converting data so that files produced in one application could be plotted in another on his hardware.

THE COLORADO RIVER:
AN INTRODUCTION

> The Colorado River is formed by the junction of the Grand and Green.
>
> —John Wesley Powell

The river we now know as the Colorado once was known as the Grand. The county that gives birth to this fourteen hundred-mile-long river still bears its original name—Grand County. Said by John Wesley Powell, head of the U.S. Geological Survey a century ago, to ". . . have its source five or six miles west of Long's Peak . . ." from there it meanders down a glacial valley and into Grand Lake. It runs with few impediments in the state of Colorado. Every river west of the Continental Divide that heads within Colorado eventually merges with the Colorado River. Unlike the majority of Colorado's better trout streams, the Colorado River is not a tailwater fishery, with the exception of one or two very short sections. Lake Granby, Shadow Mountain, and Windy Gap Reservoirs are the only impoundments on the river inside Colorado. From Granby to the Utah line only small diversion dams interfere with its westward progress. The Grand River—or the Colorado—is as close to a free-flowing stream as we will find in the state.

So what makes a tailwater fishery and why isn't the Colorado one? First, *tailwater* is an engineering term, referring to the oxygenated pool below a dam spillway or release gate. The term is used by anglers to define the section of a river below a dam and downstream runs that have similar environmental conditions to the tailwater pool. Well-known examples of tailwater fisheries include the South Platte, Fryingpan, Dolores, and Blue Rivers in Colorado. Others that could be included are the Green in Utah,

1

The Colorado River and Its Tributaries

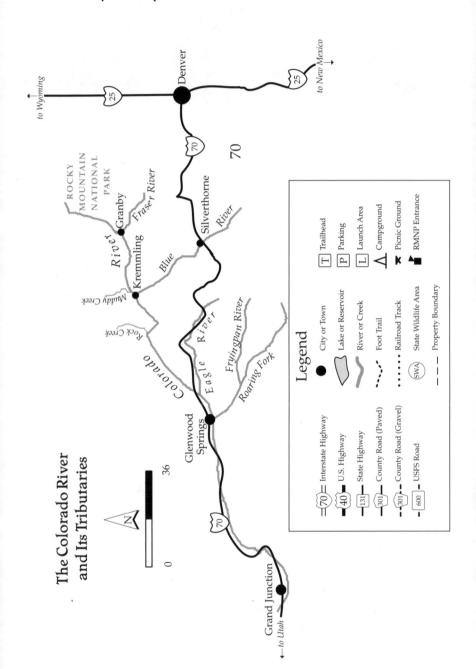

Legend

	City or Town	T	Trailhead
	Lake or Reservoir	P	Parking
	River or Creek	L	Launch Area
	Foot Trail	△	Campground
	Railroad Track	✖	Picnic Ground
SWA	State Wildlife Area	■	RMNP Entrance
	Property Boundary		

70 — Interstate Highway
40 — U.S. Highway
131 — State Highway
301 — County Road (Paved)
301 — County Road (Gravel)
600 — USFS Road

A tailwater is the highly oxygenated section of a river immediately below a dam.

New Mexico's San Juan, and the Miracle Mile section of the North Platte in Wyoming. These waters all have many things in common: Their best fisheries are located below dams; most are fed by bottom releases from the dams; the water has a relatively constant year-round temperature; because bottom-release water temperatures are above freezing, the fisheries seldom ice over; because the flows are controlled, they are less affected by runoff and the water is clear most of the year; small insects are more common, likely due to the cooler water temperatures. In a few cases, a new fishery is created downstream from a dam. The Dolores below McPhee Dam is one such case.

How long is a tailwater fishery? This varies. At the point where tributary streams dilute the clear, cold conditions of the water flowing out of a dam, typical tailwater characteristics diminish. A warmer stream merging with a tailwater fishery will increase water temperatures.

Terrain will also change the character of the stream. A river with a relatively small volume of water flowing over a broad open plain will warm faster than will a canyon river. A deep run will be less affected by the sun than will a slow, shallow, meandering section. With increasing distance from the dam, the characteristics of the tailwater fishery change to eliminate distinctive tailwater properties. That is the case with the Colorado. The only sections of the Colorado that can be considered tailwater fisheries lie below Shadow Mountain and Granby Reservoirs. The fishery below Shadow Mountain Dam is short: The river runs no more than perhaps 2 miles before entering Granby Reservoir. The second tailwater section, below Granby, offers only a quarter-mile of public water below the steep rocky slope of the road crossing the dam.

Downstream from Lake Granby the Colorado picks up the flows from Willow Creek, the Fraser River, and numerous small creeks. West of Granby, Windy Gap Reservoir is the only impediment to the river's course. The dam here is nothing more than a concrete spillway; it neither controls the flow rate nor lowers the water temperature. Between Lake Granby and Rifle, the only structures affecting the Colorado River are small diversions for irrigation and the Shoshone power plant in Glenwood Canyon.

Middle Park, named for the broad valley stretching from Winter Park at the foot of Berthoud Pass west to Kremmling, now offers the angler more than a dozen miles of water that is accessible either through CDOW or federal lands, or on private water leased by clubs or lodges. The Colorado here is classic fly-fishing water. Even Windy Gap Reservior exerts little influence on the river as far as flows are concerned. The river along this 20-or-so-mile-stretch is low gradient, with lots of riffles, meanders, and structures. Pastures and hay meadows along the banks give testimony to the nutrient-rich sediments left by the river in the past.

Near Kremmling the Colorado changes from a gentle pastoral stream to a wild one plunging deep into a granite-walled abyss.

Though they are open to recreation, Gore Canyon's Class VI rapids restrict the water to fools and expert river runners. Once past the chasm though, the river again becomes docile. From Gore Canyon downstream to Glenwood Canyon the Colorado is easily floatable, and one must be content only with a few Class II and III rapids. In Glenwood Canyon the river again turns troublesome. With Shoshone Dam, which diverts water into a Colorado Public Service generating plant, and severe rapids below, angling opportunities here are limited. At Glenwood Springs the river makes another change in character. Having joined with the Eagle at Dotsero and the Roaring Fork in Glenwood, the Colorado becomes a major river. During runoff here, the river can easily exceed 10,000 cubic feet per second (cfs).

The Colorado is a major river system. It not only collects high-country flows in its headwaters but also merges with other large rivers. These include every West Slope stream that heads within Colorado. In Grand County, the Fraser River, Willow Creek, the Williams Fork, Troublesome Creek, Muddy Creek, Blacktail Creek, and the Blue River add their waters to the Colorado. Eagle County contributes the Piney River, Rock Creek, Derby Creek, Sweetwater Creek, Deep Creek, and the Eagle River. The Roaring Fork enters the Colorado at Glenwood Springs, its flows augmented by the Fryingpan and Crystal Rivers. Although the scope of this book is limited to the waters just listed, the Colorado also picks up the Gunnison, White, Yampa, Dolores, San Juan, and Green Rivers. The list could go on.

The Ute Indians were early inhabitants of the areas surrounding the Colorado, but the geology and geography of the river was first documented by the Powell Expedition. Under the direction of the secretary of the Smithsonian Institution, John Wesley Powell led a four-year expedition to explore the Colorado beginning in 1869. The Powell Expedition was intended as a scientific investigation to observe and study the geography and geology of the river. Powell kept a daily journal on ". . . long and narrow strips of brown paper which were gathered into little volumes that were bound in sole leather . . ." He had not intended to publish his notes until the editors at *Scribner's Monthly* asked him to publish a popular account of the expedition. Four articles, illustrated with photographs taken during that four-year period, ran in *Scribner's* in 1874. That same year, Powell was called before the House Appropriations Committee to explain his work. Committee member James Garfield insisted that the history of the expedition be published. The end result is the still-available book, *The Exploration of the Colorado River and Its Canyons.*

In 1887, L. B. France published his short book of angling tales, *Rod and Line in Colorado Waters.* France possessed a sense of humor, telling of fellow anglers (a few of whom behave much as modern fishermen) driven to outdo all others by catching larger trout and greater numbers of fish. Many of his stories tell of fishing the Grand River, which we now call the Colorado. He also includes excursions to the Blue River and Williams Fork as well as to the well-known and now heavily fished South Platte.

Selected quotes from both these delightful texts and a few other sources begin selected sections of this guide to the Colorado. I hope they help you to relate to anglers of a past age who also enjoyed the river. Perhaps in some you will see yourself or fellow anglers.

Generalized hatch charts are included for rivers and sections of streams where certain hatches are of importance. Regarding such charts, remember that varying conditions affect emergence times, thus charts can only give an average time span when an insect appears. High snowpack can cause some species to emerge late or even fail to hatch in any one year. Insects also experience fluctuations in populations.

About This Guide

In the following sections of the book that describe fishing and conditions, the text is organized to make it easy to study each stretch of water. Each stream or section of a river is discussed, starting with the uppermost sections and continuing downstream. Following the descriptions of each stretch of water, sections are included entitled Access and Parking, Seasons, Equipment, and Patterns.

Access and Parking gives directions to the featured sections of a river and information on places to park. Keep in mind that access changes over time, especially when private land is involved. A stretch that was open to the public at the time this book was written may be closed by publication time. Since, in Colorado, landowners are not required to post private land, the angler is obligated to determine whether access is legal. Federal agencies at times will make land trades to improve river access in certain areas. And federal land may go into private ownership in order to gain access somewhere else. A phone call to the appropriate agency will help you determine a particular parcel's current status.

Seasons is a discussion of conditions one may expect in normal years throughout each season the river section is accessible. You will be informed regarding closures due to winter or runoff, typical water flows through the year, and water and weather conditions for each season. Though some stretches are open year-round, they may still be unfishable at times due to high water or other conditions. As much as possible, all such variables are discussed.

Equipment discusses suggested tackle, rod weights, leader-tippet sizes, wading equipment, and other items that are particularly suited to the stretch of water described. This is intended as a guide for a first visit, and recommendations are based on my personal experience and that of other anglers. None of these suggestions are to be taken as rules set in concrete.

The Patterns section is a guide to flies that are productive for most conditions. It should not be taken as an all-inclusive list. The patterns included are those that have proven effective for me and for other anglers on these waters. Naturally, there will be situations when something other than the patterns listed will take fish. If there's something to learn here, it is not to limit yourself to any list.

The 1995 Season

At times Mother Nature seems to lose track of the calendar. That appears to have been the case in the winter of 1994–95. The season began with the usual snowstorms that would dump a few inches in the high country. Time between storms was rather long though, and accumulations somewhat insignificant. By early March 1995, water districts and ski areas were wondering what had happened. Forecasters were anticipating a hot, dry summer with high fire danger. The few storms occurring toward the end of the month did little to allay concerns. Then came April.

On the day income taxes are due, the first flakes fell. Snowfall continued through June. Snowpack in the mountains ran to 400 percent of normal, and when it melted, it had to go somewhere. Stream flows in the Colorado River Basin ran high all summer and into the fall. The high flows made changes. Depending on who one asks, the changes were either beneficial or damaging. On the positive side, muck that had been accumulating for years was swept downstream. As the flows declined, new organic material was left behind, providing important nutrients for river life. On the negative side, the abnormally high water washed away the 1995 spawn.

Rivers go through cycles. The 1995 record snows were said to be a thirty-year event. Regardless of the high flows, those who fished the Colorado once the water level subsided did well. These periodic housecleaning floods likely do more good than harm in the long term.

The River That Follows the Road

All along its length, from the Continental Divide to the Utah line, the Colorado River seldom strays more than a mile or two from a road. Three highways and two county roads provide access to the river. The most direct route from the Denver metro area to the Colorado's upper and middle sections is from U.S. 40 west of Berthoud Pass. At the west end of the town of Granby, 90 miles west of Denver, head north on U.S. 34 into Rocky Mountain National Park. You can also enter the park from the east. Estes Park, west of Interstate 25, provides a scenic tour across Trail Ridge Road (U.S. 34) at elevations exceeding 2 miles. This road is open only between May and October. The National Park Service closes it as soon as the snow flies and any time there's an accumulation of more than one-eighth of an inch of snow.

West out of Granby, U.S. 40 parallels the Colorado through Middle Park on the way to the town of Kremmling. Continue west on U.S. 40 to reach Wolford Mountain Reservoir and State Highway 134 across Gore Pass to Rock Creek.

An alternate route to the Middle Park stretch is to take Interstate 70 west from Denver about 70 miles to Silverthorne. In town, take State Highway 9 south through Breckenridge to the headwaters of the Blue or north 39 miles to Kremmling and follow the Blue River Valley past Green Mountain Reservoir to the confluence with the Colorado.

One-half mile south of Kremmling, Grand County Road 1 heads west, parallel to the river but not always in sight of it. At

State Bridge, State Highway 131 runs close to the Colorado. One mile past McCoy, Eagle County Road 301 runs beside the river to Dotsero and the confluence with the Eagle River. At Silverthorne, rather than exiting Interstate 70, continue west past the town of Vail to U.S. 24 and the confluence of Gore Creek and the Eagle River. From here and all the way to Glenwood Canyon, Interstate 70 follows the Eagle while U.S. 6, a two-lane highway, gives access to the river.

From Glenwood Canyon west to Rifle, Interstate 70 takes you beside the Colorado. West of Glenwood Springs, U.S. 6 and county roads give access to parking areas along the river.

At Glenwood Springs, State Highway 82 heads south to Aspen, following the Roaring Fork all the way to its headwaters. From Basalt, Eagle County Road 104 runs beside the Fryingpan to Reudi Reservoir.

THE WAY OF A RIVER

And so my eyes wander from this product of nature's great lapidary over to the waterfall and the mountain gorge, which had been his workshop, how many thousand years ago, who can tell?
    —L. B. France, *With Rod and Line in Colorado Waters*

A nglers tend to take rivers for granted. Whether to the Colorado or another river we go fishing, expecting to catch the trout we know are there. Few give any thought to the river itself. Perhaps we view it only as a trout's home. We all know that various structures in the river provide feeding, resting, or spawning habitat for the fish. Have you ever taken a look at a cutbank, say, and wondered about it? Why is it there? Why do rivers meander, following sinuously curved courses, rather than run in a straight line? What causes a river to take the form it does?

As an angler, I see the habitat in the Colorado. A large boulder offers protection from a raging current. Gravel provides a place to spawn. Shallow riffles attract fish to emerging insects. A deep cut bank is home to a large brown. As a geologist, I see the Colorado as a dynamic system. Its character changes more frequently and more quickly than a lake or reservoir does. One day it runs low and clear. The next, runoff swells its channel, overflowing the banks. One year a river may follow one course, in the next it has carved a new path.

Let's take a quick look at the river. We'll examine how it works and perhaps explain the reasons why some parts hold fish and others are nearly barren.

Rivers have one purpose: to transport sediment. Elements of nature are continually at work wearing down the Rockies. Boulders

11

are broken down to smaller and smaller particles, eventually becoming sand and even finer grains. In time, the boulder resting in the Colorado's headwaters is reduced in size and its grains carried away to the Gulf of California. The Colorado River is a dynamic system that is constantly changing; it has many different moods. In this process of change, debris is eroded, moved, sorted, deposited, reworked, and moved again. Structures are created, then destroyed. Channels are scoured, then filled. Some changes occur rapidly; others are almost imperceptible.

In the Tertiary period, roughly fifty million years ago, the Rocky Mountains were under construction. The range went through a period of uplift, was worn down, then was uplifted again. Following the last uplift, glaciers went to work scouring the cliffs, forming the sharp peaks and deep valleys. When the glaciers receded, the Continental Divide and the Front Range were left in nearly their present configuration. But nature's construction projects are never-ending. As soon as she builds a mountain range, she begins tearing it down. Freezing and thawing cycles crack the granites and metamorphic rocks exposed above timberline. Melting snows collect in fractures and begin a downhill journey. Flows from hundreds of rivulets merge into a few, then into a single channel, carrying weathered rock fragments.

With time and distance, a river's profile changes. The channel becomes less steep and is made deeper and broader. What began as a trickle grows into a major river system. The suspended particle load in the current also increases. At a stream's head the particle size is too large for the water to do much with it, and the current gradually moves it along the bed. But at high water flows during runoff, surprisingly large rocks get moved.

As would be expected, rocks that line the Colorado's bed are largest near the river's head. The water's tumbling action soon reduces boulders to cobbles, then cobbles are broken into pebbles. With time and distance, everything is eventually ground into sand, then to even finer particles that are so tiny that even a slight current prevents settling.

After leaving the high mountains, the Colorado enters the gentle valley of Middle Park and changes character. Near Granby the river takes the flows from the Fraser River and Willow Creek. Middle Park, a broad valley, gives the river room to move back and forth. Here, another environment dominates. The river's gradient becomes gentle, the current less powerful. As the stream meanders, larger material settles on the bed. Large boulders find a nearly stable position and become fish-holding structures. Bends and pools are established. Quiet water alternates with riffles.

In a lower-elevation environment, the river changes again. Each place the river enters a basin, be it an ocean or a reservoir, the channel broadens. It also becomes shallow in proportion to its width. That's because the sediment load has changed considerably, becoming fine enough to be carried in suspension. The reduced speed of the current has let heavier material drop out, changing the depth-to-width ratio. Wide meanders build a broad depositional area. The closer the river gets to the basin, the slower it moves and the more sediment it dumps. At these places the sediment is fine enough to be worked more easily by the current, and the area eventually takes on a delta-like appearance. Such places are usually great fish-holding areas. Reduced current speed means a fish will find it easier to hold in position in order to gather an abundance of food coming its way.

Let's go back upstream for a bit. Most rivers begin with a steep slope, as you will find in the Colorado's headwaters in Rocky Mountain National Park. In the middle, the slope lessens and the channel enlarges. This is the character of the Colorado in Middle Park. The lower portion runs over a nearly level bed as it approaches an impoundment or sea level. The channel becomes even broader and proportionately shallower. Near Kremmling, and again between Gore and Glenwood Canyons, the Colorado behaves similarly to a stream entering a basin as the narrow canyon walls restrict the river's current.

If nothing had happened geologically west of the Continental Divide, the Colorado would follow a typical stream profile all the way to the Gulf. But a process called *rejuvenation* periodically renews the river's channel. In rejuvenation an area of land is uplifted and the process of erosion begins anew.

In Gore Canyon, downstream from State Highway 9 near Kremmling, you will find another example of mountain building. Rejuvenation took place here with the geological thrusting that built the Williams Fork Range, east of Green Mountain Reservoir. Here, as in Rocky Mountain National Park, very old rock—over a billion years old—was pushed from beneath the earth to the surface. On top of Wolford Mountain, 6 miles north of Kremmling, you can see the results of all the tugging, pulling, pushing, and squeezing. Notice that the lower half of the mountain is barren, covered only by grasses and low brush. The upper half, though, is a forest of evergreens growing out of the soils that were eroded from ancient granites that covered the ancient rock.

After this thrusting occurred, Gore Canyon came into existence. The river followed a fracture system in the rocks that was established eons earlier. Only now, the Colorado flows through the uplifted rock, which is highly resistant to erosion. The result is a rubble-filled bed creating nearly impassable rapids in the narrow canyon. You'll find the same situation in much more spectacular form in Glenwood Canyon.

As we've seen, in the Colorado's upper course the predominant geological feature is erosion. The terrain is high and steep. Elements of nature—wind, freeze-thaw cycles, and gravity—all work to wear down the most resistant rock. The particles of rock soon make their way into the river channel, where the water begins transporting it to lower elevations.

We've also seen that the Colorado runs through valleys, as do all streams. Over time the valleys deepen and become broader, the result of the river's tendency to meander. This brings up a question: Why do rivers meander?

A streambed has irregularities that can be large or small. They serve to deflect the current, forcing it away from themselves. This causes the current to wear away the bank opposite the deflection. As the one bank is being eroded, the current on the other bank is slowed, which allows it to deposit sediment. This gradually shifts the channel, let's assume to the left. As the left bank gets cut, the right bank fills. The water's velocity on the left side increases. The increased velocity into the bank deflects the current to the right as it moves downstream, and it then begins to cut away on the right bank. Over time, a channel that was once straight becomes a series of sinuous curves. An aerial view of Middle Park shows a stream that is much longer than the length of the valley due to a meandering channel.

That's only one view of the cause of meanders. Some scientists conclude that a river will meander because this is the most efficient way for it to do its job with the least expenditure of energy. Although bottom irregularities will induce a wave pattern in a river's channel, they are not essential for meanders to occur, according to alternate theories.

Let's take a look at how to fish a meander. The inside part of a bend, or meander, is an area of deposition. The water's energy is lowest here, and heavy sediment—sand, pebbles, and some larger rocks—are deposited. This is also the shallowest part of the channel. Because the point bar is growing away from the river's bank, less cover for trout exists. Streamside brush can't shade the bar. No large boulders are found. A trout can't hide here, and fish are usually found in this part of the channel only during a hatch, or at dark, when they are less exposed to predators. How do you recognize a point bar? It's the gravelly area on the inside of a river's bend that is devoid of vegetation. Its sediment is unconsolidated and shifts easily under your feet. During runoff, the bar is under water.

The point bar on the left is an area of deposition. The river's energy erodes the bank on the opposite side, the cut bank on the right.

Now, let's move out into the channel, toward the middle. The water is deepest here, the current stronger. This area moves the most material, be it sediment, debris, or trout food. Opposite the point bar is the cutbank. Unlike the bar, the cutbank is an area of erosion. The channel is still deep, though not as deep as in the middle portion.

In a few places, the river erodes deep cuts into the bank well back from the main current. Vegetation is sometimes all that holds such banks together. Grass or willows shade the hole made by the current. This gives big browns a hiding place. The nearby deep current carries an abundance of insects, nymphs, and small fish. It should be no surprise that this area will attract the larger fish: A trout must have sufficient muscle mass to rush out into the strong current and then quickly return to its hole.

Though it may not appear so at first glance, riffles have much in common with meanders. On the surface, riffle water appears uniformly rippled. A study of the bottom, though, reveals subtle variations. Boulders, even those that are completely covered, deflect faster currents to their sides. Immediately downstream of these obstructions the water's energy is reduced, sediment is deposited. On the bottom, miniature channels are created that act much like the larger structures associated with meanders. The Colorado's riffles, such as those you'll fish on the Breeze or Sunset properties, have hundreds of these small fish-holding structures. Visit the river at low flow, in late summer. The clear water reveals these small variations in the bottom current. Remember these places and drift a nymph through them when the flows are higher.

While a river creates meanders, it also deepens its valley. At the same time, the meanders move downstream. The next time you fish the Breeze property near Parshall, observe that the path from the parking area leads across a broad flat above the river. Look across to the south side and you will see a similar flat at the same height above the water. This feature is called a *terrace*. It once was the level of the river's channel. Notice also the breadth of the valley. This also defines the extent of the past course of the river as it wandered back and forth—widening, cutting down, and deepening its channel. In a few places you will find channels that are no longer a part of the river. These will be off to the side, usually near a meander. This is a place where the river has created a new channel and cut off the old channel that is now connected to the river only by a small trickle feeding into what is called an "oxbow lake." It demonstrates the dynamic nature of a river and its constantly changing nature.

A river is affected not only by geological events but also by structures, natural and artificial, and by seasonal occurrences. Structures—anything that causes a variation in the water's flow—affect water chemistry. It's reasonable to assume that a river such as the Colorado is saturated with oxygen and other atmospheric gases. This enrichment occurs at places of turbulence. Plunges from falls, spillways, and other structures add air to and mix it with the water. Although, in general, this is good for the trout, negative side effects can also occur. For instance, nitrogen is a major component of the atmosphere. In 1994, CDOW biologists found fingerling trout that appeared to be suffering from excess nitrogen gas in the water just west of Granby. Trout have been found with symptoms such as an over-inflated swim bladder, distended eyes, suppressed immunity, reduced growth, and loss of swimming ability. The source of the excess nitrogen in this water is thought to come from the Windy Gap Reservoir spillway. The problem lessens going downstream through Middle Park.

One event we're all familiar with is the spring runoff, and it's the phenomenon that influences most greatly the way of a river. Let's take a look at the hydrologic cycle and see how it affects a river system. We'll begin with the winter season on the Colorado.

It comes as no surprise that winter finds the Colorado with a covering of ice. Here and there through Middle Park the river has short runs that remain open, but even those are carrying slush. Downstream from Glenwood Springs the Colorado seldom freezes over, though ice may form along the banks. Beneath the ice, the current still flows at its annual minimum rate. Temperatures are low—an insignificant number of degrees above freezing. Fish move into deeper holes to shiver through the cold.

In spring the days become longer, so more sunlight hits the ice, converting it to liquid. Temperatures climb as winter releases its icy grip on the landscape. Once again we find running water in the Colorado. At last we can go fishing. This period presents the angler with some good fishing in Middle Park.

For a period of one to two months the river flows low and clear, though a bit cold. By late April most of the snow at lower elevations has melted. At places such as the confluence with the Williams Fork at Parshall, warm daytime temperatures melt enough snow to discolor the water. The high country, though, is still frozen, so these small influxes have little effect on the overall volume of water.

In normal years high-country snow begins to melt usually in May, and with the melting comes the high water we all dread. This is another time of year in which we seek other places to wet a line. Peak flows of eight to ten times the late summer or fall flows occur at this time. Without this event the river would stagnate. Sediment and trash that has accumulated through the year is flushed away now, renewing the riverbed. Nutrients that feed bottom-dwelling organisms are replaced during this annual event. Perhaps we should see runoff not with disdain but as spring housecleaning, something that's necessary to maintain the fishery. In the area near Hot Sulphur Springs, runoff can offer good angling, provided the flows are reasonable. Even at 600 cfs you'll still get into fish along the edges.

After peaking, the flow begins a steady decline and settles down to the low and clear conditions of summer. This period is characterized by slowly declining flows interrupted at times by rains that may temporarily raise current levels and discolor the water. Temperatures stabilize too, stimulating insect hatches and trout feeding frenzies.

With fall comes even lower flows. The water begins to cool, insect hatches are sparse, and the fish activity occurs mostly during midday and the afternoon. One thing to remember about the Colorado is that, unlike tailwater fisheries, the flow is largely uncontrolled. Therefore, conditions are more variable throughout the year than will be seen downstream from dams on other rivers.

The Colorado River is really many rivers, with a different character in each of its different sections. Becoming familiar with the river is like a good marriage: The longer the relationship lasts, the better it becomes. Once you get to know the Colorado, you will come to love it in each of its moods.

ROCKY MOUNTAIN NATIONAL PARK

The Colorado River originates in Rocky Mountain National Park beneath the Continental Divide near a place called La Poudre Pass. No more than a high mountain creek at first, it starts its journey to the Gulf of California at the edge of a 10,200-foot-high meadow. In the first mile it adds the flows of Bennet and Specimen Creeks, along with other unnamed streams. From here, the Colorado plunges downstream past historic sites once the domain of ancient peoples of the Clovis culture, and later Plains Indian tribes, miners, summer tourists, and anglers.

In the first 3 miles of its existence the Colorado drops 900 feet. In the Kawuneeche Valley, 5 miles downstream from its beginning, the Colorado becomes a stream worthy of tempting an angler to drift a dry fly. The glacial river valley opens, allowing the river to meander over the broad, nearly level floodplain. In 8 miles through the Kawuneeche Valley the Colorado probably runs twice that distance due to its many meanders.

Northwest of the town of Grand Lake the Colorado exits the park and flows through private land until it enters Shadow Mountain Lake. Below this reservoir the river is large, with more than a mile of stream to fish.

The river at one time had two forks, the North and the South. The North Fork of the Colorado, which is the only remaining headwater of the Colorado, will be found on older topographic and Forest Service maps. The South Fork, formed by Arapaho, Buchanan, and Cascade Creeks, is now buried beneath Monarch Lake and Lake Granby. The forks merged near the confluence with Willow Creek. All that's left of the South Fork is a short

21

stretch, less than a mile in length, between the two reservoirs. Arapaho, Buchanan, and Cascade are small high-country streams with small fish. Regardless of the less-than-exciting angling there, you will find the trails leading to the upper stretches quite busy. The old North Fork runs into Shadow Mountain Lake on the west side of the reservoir, and from there the last park section of the Colorado flows into Lake Granby.

Grand Lake is Colorado's largest natural body of water. It's also deep—about 300 feet to the bottom. Shadow Mountain and Granby are reservoirs. All three lakes have rainbow, brown, and Mackinaw trout, along with kokanee salmon. Probably the best fly-fishing opportunities here will be the shallows in early morning and late evening. Shoreline access is difficult around Grand Lake due to the preponderance of private property. The west shoreline of Shadow Mountain has much the same situation. The south and east sides offer better access. In Lake Granby, anglers will find irresistible temptation in the shallows of Rainbow Bay. Belly boaters should take advantage of this easy-to-access fishing along U.S. 34. Monarch Lake is shallow, and CDOW records indicate it holds rainbow, brook, brown, and cutthroat trout to 12 inches, with brookies being caught most frequently.

Ambitious hikers will find more than a few high lakes in the Colorado drainage to fish within Rocky Mountain National Park. The Timber Creek, Onahu Creek, and Tonahu Creek Trails lead to backcountry lakes from U.S. 34 north of Grand Lake. North from the town of Grand Lake, by the filtration plant, the North Inlet Trail and the East Inlet Trail both reach scattered backcountry lakes. Several are above timberline. Check with park rangers for fishing information and special regulations. You will need a valid Colorado fishing license in the park. Fishing regulations in the park may vary from those in the rest of the state. Overnight stays in the backcountry require a permit.

The Kawuneeche Valley

In the Kawuneeche Valley 3 miles downstream from Lulu City the Colorado settles into a meandering meadow stream, the first place worth drifting a fly through riffles and pools. The river's still small here, 20 to 30 feet across, and easy to fish. Creeks merging with the main stream and beaver ponds are good places to try for brookies. Because such places are usually easy to fish, this is a good area in which to get a kid or new angler into the sport of fly fishing.

Throughout its 8 miles in the Kawuneeche Valley, the river's low gradient induces the current to work slowly at eroding the unconsolidated sediments, creating meanders. At each bend the channel along the cutbank deepens into trout-holding pools. Here and there you'll find debris carried down by high flows from spring runoff, and logjams created by the annual torrents from deep holes. That's more fish habitat. This is a small stream, and small-stream tactics apply. With low, clear water conditions following runoff, you'll want to keep a low profile to avoid spooking fish.

The size of the fish in the Kawuneeche Valley is perhaps the greatest surprise awaiting the fly fisherman. Browns to 16 inches, and some larger, inhabit the deep holes. Though these fish are usually eager to take a fly or nymph, early fall is a good time to try for the browns because they're spawning then. Of course, you'll find the ubiquitous brookies, and for the most part they'll be small. Rainbows also swim here. Midsummer is the best time to hook into one, although in years with light snow cover, the pre-runoff period can offer good rainbow fishing.

The river bottom is alive with insect larvae. Most of what you will find from turning over rocks is small, as should be your patterns. Not much out of the ordinary is needed, though. Stock your

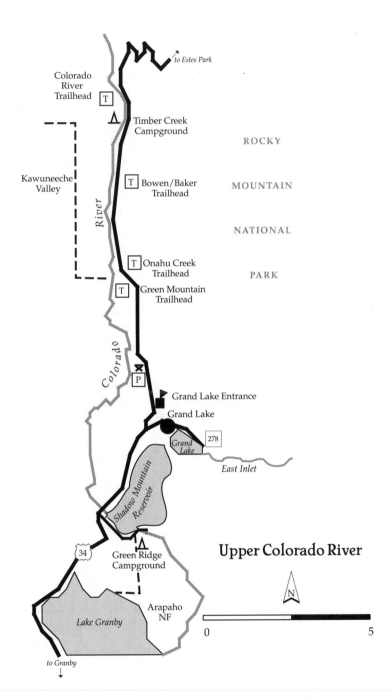

Colorado River Trailhead [T]

to Estes Park

△ Timber Creek Campground

ROCKY

Kawuneeche Valley

[T] Bowen/Baker Trailhead

MOUNTAIN

River

NATIONAL

[T] Onahu Creek Trailhead

[T] Green Mountain Trailhead

PARK

Colorado

[P]

Grand Lake Entrance

Grand Lake

Grand Lake

278

East Inlet

Shadow Mountain Reservoir

34

△ Green Ridge Campground

Upper Colorado River

N

Arapaho NF

Lake Granby

0   5

to Granby

fly box with an assortment of drys: Blue-Winged Olives, Elkhair Caddis, Humpys, Pale Morning Duns, Red Quills, Royal Wulffs, Adamses, Adams Irresistibles, Griffith Gnats, and such. Small sizes will be most useful, 16 down to 20. Nymph patterns should also be small. You'll want a few Gold-Ribbed Hare's Ears in various colors. Make sure to include a few in smaller sizes tied with Krystal Flash wingcases to imitate *Baetis* emergers. Stock up on your favorite caddis and midge larva imitations. Tie up a few generic mayfly nymphs just in case. Throw in a few small Breadcrusts, too.

Following a broad glacial valley down from the high slopes through the Kawuneeche Valley in the park, the terrain is easy to walk. Most of the plain along the river is timbered, and though you'll encounter a few steep banks, there's usually a way around them. Elevation in the Kawuneeche Valley is about 8,800 feet, and around 8,300 feet below Shadow Mountain Dam.

Rocky Mountain National Park enforces fishing regulations on the Colorado in the park. You must purchase an entrance pass, which is required most days of the year. The fee gets you park access for seven days and is available at all park gates. An annual parks pass, which applies in all national parks, can be purchased at any park entrance or from National Park Service offices. Dogs are permitted only in roadside campgrounds and must be on a leash at all times. You will need a permit for park travel if you plan to stay overnight in the backcountry. The permits are available at the park or can be purchased in advance. For information, call the Rocky Mountain National Park headquarters, (970) 586-1399.

Fishing in most park waters is restricted to flies and lures, and it is strictly catch-and-release for browns, cutthroats, and rainbows. Children under twelve are permitted to use bait but only in waters not restricted to catch-and-release angling. Check with park personnel regarding the restrictions. A valid Colorado fishing license is required, and the park does not require any additional permits other than the state license.

Although your main purpose may be fishing, don't let that distract you from the natural wonders. Rocky Mountain National Park has abundant wildlife. You'll run across mule deer, elk, black bear, and moose in areas along the river and U.S. 34. The animals are seldom bothered by hunters unless they wander outside the park and are accustomed to people as no more than camera-toting annoyances. Moose were introduced into Colorado in the late 1970s and have done well in this section of the park. If you do come across one, don't argue over who has the right-of-way. Be especially careful around moose at any time and around elk during the rut—from late August through early November. Black bears may snoop around your camp. Store your food properly in bearproof containers and avoid cooking inside your tent.

Trails away from roads give you a chance to view bighorn sheep as well as the many small critters that inhabit the alpine regions of the park. You'll find wildflowers everywhere. Take a camera, for fishing's not the only thing to enjoy here.

~ Access and Parking

Inside the park, fishing access is by foot only, and there is no handicap access due to the nature of the trails and streambanks. The lower Kawuneeche Valley can be reached from several picnic grounds and parking areas north of the west entrance. Trailhead and picnic ground parking provides access to the river at the Green Mountain, Onahu Creek, Bowen/Baker, and Colorado River trailheads. If you stay at Timber Creek Campground, you will also have access there.

The headwaters of the river is accessed by a hiking trail leaving from the Colorado River trailhead. The path meanders uphill through Shipler Park, past the remnants of an old mining town—Lulu City—and up toward the Continental Divide.

The Colorado forms about 4 meandering miles (it would be about 3 miles in a straight line) of the park's western boundary in the Kawuneeche Valley. The west bank is within Arapaho National Forest, though the land along that bank is private. This means you may walk only along the east bank or in the river. Step out on the west bank and you'll be trespassing. One must pay attention here, because not all private property is posted.

In spite of the private holdings along the river, when you get out of sight of homes and guest ranches in the area you can easily feel as though you are in the middle of uncharted wilderness. That's due in part to the nature of the river, which runs free in its natural state. Though traffic on U.S. 34 passes by a half-mile in the distance, most of the sound is absorbed by the pine forest. It gives one a feeling of solitude in the midst of incredible beauty.

You have several options for fishing the upper Colorado River in the Kawuneeche Valley. One is to park at the picnic ground $1\frac{1}{2}$ miles north of the Grand Lake entrance north of Granby. From the parking lot, several unmarked trails lead through the timber to the river, which flows about one-half mile west of the road.

As is typical of the river in the Kawuneeche Valley, the meanders are broken occasionally by short smooth runs and riffled pools that don't often tax an angler's wading ability. The banks are open, seldom presenting an obstacle to your backcast. A lightly worn path follows the east bank of the river.

From the picnic ground one can fish one's way upstream more than 2 miles, at which point the river runs close to the highway. Once at the blacktop, you can walk back to your car. Murphy and I like to carry along a pair of sneakers in our vests or daypacks so that we don't have to make that walk wearing hip boots. Remember that even though the highway distance is about 2 miles, by river it's considerably more due to the countless meanders. Allow a full day to fish this section. For those who feel uncomfortable touring unfamiliar country, pick up a topo of the area or follow the map available at any park entrance.

In another mile north, you can park at the Green Mountain trailhead, or at Onahu Creek trailhead, a half-mile still farther. Continue north another 3 miles to the Bowen/Baker trailhead and picnic ground. A mile north of Bowen/Baker and just east of the Never Summer Ranch is another picnic ground. Should you camp at Timber Creek Campground, a half-mile farther up the valley, you will be within a few feet of the river. In the next mile and a half are two more picnic grounds and the Colorado River trailhead, all of which have parking for river access. You may not park along the road shoulder.

➤ Seasons

In the spring, much river access is determined by Mother Nature. Although the park is open year-round, the river isn't. At best, you'll be able to fish the Kawuneeche Valley as early as April, though this early season will be interrupted by runoff. Because snows can accumulate to considerable depth on the Divide, the river is often high and roily from late May through early June.

Summer brings out the best hatches and most pleasant weather from late June through August. Following runoff the river runs low and clear, and it is easy to wade. A red quill hatch occurs in midsummer. Most often, though, it's best to fish proven patterns rather than to worry about matching specific insects.

Fall fishing, in September and October, is primarily for browns as they work their way upstream to spawn in the river's gravel beds. Late-season conditions here can be deceiving. With low and clear water, even the smaller fish can require a delicate presentation and long casts. Fine tippets are helpful too. 5X may be too large. Should you choose a 7X or smaller, tie on some of the new superstrength materials in case you hook one of the larger browns. A good-quality 6X tippet should work fine.

➤ Equipment

A small, light rod, say a 1- to 3-weight, is ideal for the Kawuneeche Valley in the park. The insects run small here, so tippets of 5X and smaller are advised—not necessarily because the fish are leadershy but to fit through the eyes of tiny patterns. You will want to use high-strength material to handle the occasional 16-inch brown you'll take. Because the stream is small, hip waders will be adequate for all seasons other than during runoff. Thundershowers occur frequently in the park due to the mountainous terrain, so it's always advisable to have a rain parka along. A light daypack is useful to carry assorted items and lunch.

➤ Patterns

Insects and nymphs tend to be small in the upper river through the park. Suggested patterns include but are not limited to Blue-Winged Olive, Pale Morning Dun, Elkhair Caddis, Humpy, Adams, Adams Irresistible, Griffith Gnat, Pheasant Tail, Gold-Ribbed Hare's Ear, midge and caddis larvae, midge emergers, ants, and grasshoppers.

Small streams have given me some of my most enjoyable fishing. Until my friend Murphy suggested a day trip to the upper Colorado in the Kawuneeche Valley, though, I had never thought of the Colorado as a small stream. In late summer the river is little more than a creek. Even wearing hip waders, an angler is rarely in danger of going in so deep as to risk getting wet. In some places one can wade in the river through water barely over the ankles. The few deep pools are easy to bypass. To see the river in summer makes it difficult to associate it with the monstrous flows past State Bridge and Burns or with the roaring current in Glenwood Canyon during spring runoff.

We had the Kawuneeche Valley to ourselves that late-autumn day. That's one advantage of fishing the late season in Rocky

Mountain National Park: Summer vacations are over, and few tourists venture into the park then. Murphy's truck was the only vehicle in the picnic ground a mile and a half north of the Grand Lake Entrance Station. In spite of the cold, the river ran free of ice—clear but frigid.

The day slowly warmed, awakening the browns. Being most familiar with the river, Murphy had the best luck—several fish over 12 inches. On a dry fly, too. We did find, to our dismay, that we were a bit late to get in on the fall spawning run of browns out of Shadow Mountain Reservoir.

The fish didn't cooperate all that well for me. By midafternoon, I was ready to leave. Unfortunately, Murphy had driven, and his truck keys were tucked safely in his jeans pocket. To pass the time for a while, I climbed a high bank and spotted fish in the crystal-clear stream. One fish I had directed him to, a brown of perhaps 14 inches, was attracted by a Royal Wulff. From overhead, I watched as the fish first examined the fly, then drifted backward beneath it. The brown opened his mouth to partake of the enticement. Too quickly though, Murphy set the hook, barely missing the nice fish.

Encouraged by the increasing number of rising fish, I went to work on a downstream brown. I cast the fly into the head of a slow-moving flat pool and let the current take the #18 Adams Irresistible to the dimpling fish. After a few drifts, the 12-incher took. My season was complete.

Shadow Mountain Dam Tailwater

The Colorado forms a boundary of Rocky Mountain National Park in another place. Between Shadow Mountain Dam and the inlet to Lake Granby there are about 2 miles of tailwater angling.

The river is much larger here. Check the flows before making the trip to this section; water releases can make the river difficult or impossible to wade.

You'll find a smorgasbord of fish here: browns, rainbows, and Mackinaw. The Mackinaw trout can make for exciting fishing, and this is one of the few spots on the river where you have a chance to take one on a fly. The Macs are usually taken while an angler is trying for a brown or rainbow.

Immediately below the spillway are some good structures to work. Large boulders offer holding places for trout. Along the left bank is a large backwater eddy. Downstream, the river's gradient is high, the current fast. You'll find lots of rocks to provide cover. The banks are lined with tall willows, so in most places one has to wade out into the tricky currents to fish. Be aware that you will find few places from which to cross the river, even at low flows. This is also a popular stretch of water. On weekends you'll find it quite busy.

If you plan an extended visit to the area, camping is an option for overnight stays. Within the park and in the areas around Lake Granby, Shadow Mountain Lake, and Grand Lake, you'll find campgrounds. Lodging and meals are available in the town of Grand Lake, and in Granby, which is 24 miles to the south of the park. Fishing information and tackle can be found in both towns.

The U.S. Forest Service manages the public land along rivers and lakes outside the park. Colorado Division of Wildlife regulations regarding angling methods and limits apply below Shadow Mountain Dam. Between Shadow Mountain Dam and Granby Reservoir, fishing is closed between October 15 and December 31. Special regulations regarding bag and possession limits are in place on Mackinaw and splake (a brook-Mackinaw hybrid). Check the current issue of the *Colorado Fishing Season Information and Wildlife Property Directory*, because regulations change periodically.

The Colorado River below Shadow Mountain Dam.

The short stretch of river below Shadow Mountain Dam is the only tailwater section of the Colorado in the state that is suitable for fly fishing. Even so, it's not really a year-round fishery. Winter temperatures in the valley drop low enough to freeze the mercury in thermometers. Water releases at other times can be unpredictable. Check WaterTalk (see pages 152–153) or call Nelson Fly & Tackle Shop in Tabernash for information: (970) 726-8558.

➻ Access and Parking

To get to the tailwater, 2 miles north of Lake Granby take the Shadow Mountain Dam access road east. There are parking areas near the dam, and from them you can walk downstream along either side of the river.

The Colorado enters Shadow Mountain from the west. Between the inlet and the park boundary upstream no public access is available because the land is held privately.

➤ Seasons

The best times to try this section are prior to runoff in the spring, and then in summer, following the high-water season. The river between the Shadow Mountain Spillway and Granby is closed to angling from October 15 through December 31.

➤ Equipment

Your favorite 4- to 6-weight rod will be fine here. Along with chest waders you may want a wading staff, for the current can be strong and the bottom slippery.

➤ Patterns

In addition to the patterns listed for the Kawuneeche Valley, try Woolly Buggers and Muddler Minnows. Although this book is a guide to fly fishing the Colorado, be aware that in this section all angling methods are legal. Hardware may be more productive here due to the width and depth of the tailwater pool.

FRASER RIVER

The Fraser heads beneath the west side of Berthoud Pass at an elevation of more than 11,000 feet. It rapidly descends the pass's narrow, steep-sided valley. At the town of Fraser the river is down to 8,800 feet. Through the canyon northwest of Tabernash its course is at 8,200 feet, and it joins the Colorado west of Granby at 7,900 feet.

The river varies in character from a meandering meadow stream near Tabernash to a rushing mountain river in a few other places. The Fraser averages perhaps 50 feet in width. In spots it's too deep to easily wade across, but most of it won't give anglers any great difficulty. Along the Southern Pacific Railroad right-of-way the river runs through a narrow gorge. Here the banks are steep along both sides.

This river has never received the kind of attention that Colorado's more famous rivers do. It does, however, offer the angler different water in which to wet a fly. The Fraser is worth a try by anyone looking for something other than the busier streams. It's rarely overcrowded. In the upper meadow section, long meanders give the angler plenty of river to fish. Brush along the banks here and there provides cover for the trout yet doesn't present too many opportunities to snag a fly. Scattered boulders also provide cover and feeding stations for fish.

Coming off the Continental Divide the Fraser is a small, brush-lined high-mountain stream holding mostly small brookies and rainbows. Near the community of Tabernash the river takes on the character of a proper trout stream. It's populated here with brooks, browns, cutthroats, and rainbows. Jim Nelson, who with

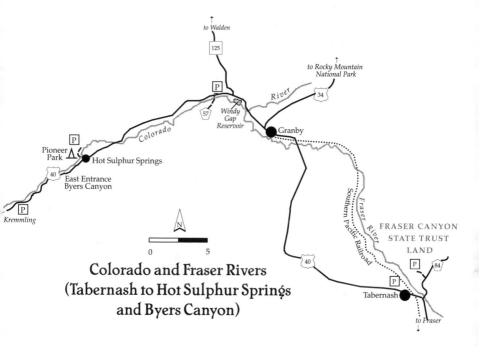

to Walden

125

to Rocky Mountain
National Park

P

River

34

57 Windy
Gap
Reservoir

Granby

P

Colorado

Pioneer
Park Hot Sulphur Springs

40 East Entrance
Byers Canyon

P

Kremmling

N

Southern Pacific Railroad

Fraser River

FRASER CANYON
STATE TRUST
LAND

P

84

0   5

P

40

Tabernash

**Colorado and Fraser Rivers
(Tabernash to Hot Sulphur Springs
and Byers Canyon)**

to Fraser

his wife Kathy operates Nelson Fly & Tackle Shop in Tabernash, says these are wild trout, and one of 16 inches is a good fish. Murphy tells of seeing rainbows to 20 inches in the river.

Along the 16 miles of river in Fraser Canyon between Tabernash and Granby the land is a mix of Forest Service (USFS), Bureau of Land Management (BLM), and private ownership. The CDOW manages the river between Meadow Creek and Granby as Wild Trout Water. There are no restrictions on angling method, but there is a limit of two fish.

The Fraser is one of Murphy's favorite rivers, and he fishes it often. In his experience, the fish tend to concentrate in the deeper holes and runs rather than being distributed throughout the stream. He suggests casting a fly along the banks, around plunge pools, and below fast narrow chutes.

The Fraser River offers excellent summer dry-fly fishing.

ᕙ Access and Parking

U.S. 40 meets the headwaters of the Fraser a few miles west of Berthoud Pass. Campgrounds and pullouts provide access to the upper river. West of Winter Park there is no public access to the river until you reach Tabernash.

Until recently, anglers accessed the Fraser from an unmarked road west of Tabernash. With the opening of the Fraser Canyon State Trust Land (STL) unit north of town, anglers can avoid trespassing on Southern Pacific (formerly the Denver and Rio Grande Western) right-of-way. East of Tabernash, go 0.5 mile north on Grand County Road 84 to Strawberry Road, then 1.5 miles northwest to the property. Use caution if you fish downstream through the canyon along the railroad track—trains do pass through here several times each day.

➤ Seasons

Nelson says spring fishing on the river can be good toward the end of April through the beginning of the runoff in May. Caddis and mayflies make up most of the insects on the river then. High water usually lasts until late June.

July and August are the prime summer months. Caddis, mayflies, midges, and small stoneflies are abundant at that time. Nelson suggests that anglers study the life on the stream bottom, then use appropriate matching patterns, usually the same imitations anglers find effective on other Middle Park rivers.

Though the fishing is still good as fall arrives, by September the river is fairly quiet, because fewer anglers try their luck then. You can fish into October, though cooler temperatures slow the action a bit. Attractor patterns will induce the most action. Nymphs will also get strikes. Try small Gold-Ribbed Hare's Ears or peacock herl patterns.

➤ Equipment

The Fraser is a great river for light tackle. Most fish range from 10 to 16 inches, and a 2- through 4-weight rod 7 to 9 feet in length will handle the fish and water conditions.

At times other than runoff, hip waders will allow access to most of the river. A few deep holes will be easier to wade in chest waders, but these can be avoided if you prefer to use hippers or waist-high waders.

➤ Patterns

Murphy favors small attractor patterns such as a Royal Wulff or Adams Irresistible here. Nymphers might want to try an olive Hare's Ear with a Flashback wingcase fished as an emerger. For imitating small stoneflies, any of the peacock herl body patterns should be good, such as Prince Nymphs or Halfbacks. Fish them in sizes 14 and smaller.

On a windy March day Murphy and I gave up fighting 50-mile-an-hour gusts with 4-weight rods and headed home through Middle Park. As we approached Tabernash, Murphy suggested we pull in at Nelson Fly & Tackle Shop. Jim and Kathy Nelson own the only fly shop in Colorado that still operates under its original ownership after twenty-five years. Jim finished helping a customer from Kansas and then greeted the two of us.

A few minutes later Jim headed to the back of the store and pulled out a 1953 edition of *Collier's* magazine that was opened to a three-page story about President Eisenhower fishing in the area. I had long thought he fished the Fraser when staying at the Byers Peak Ranch. But he cast flies into St. Louis Creek, which joins the Fraser near the ranch.

The story mentioned that Ike's favorite fly was a House and Lot, a pattern that greatly resembles a Royal Wulff. If this one didn't produce, he would switch to a Rio Grande King, Red Variant, or Ginger Quill. This was only a few years after Ernest Schwiebert wrote *Matching The Hatch*; fishing with exact imitations had not yet caught on with fly fishermen.

The president did have good luck on the tributary of the Fraser. One reason for his success, as reported by the *Collier's* writer, had to do with area sportsmen's clubs stocking the creek with 15-inch rainbows before Ike arrived. The writer reported that the president had good luck fishing but would at times miss a strike. At such times, Ike was able to call upon a vocabulary cultivated by his forty years of army service to properly address the situation.

Is it possible that we can be grateful to a past president of the United States for the existing fishery in the Fraser? Who knows? It's a pleasant thought, though, to consider that a few of the trout we now find in the Fraser descended from those stockings in St. Louis Creek forty years ago.

MIDDLE PARK: GRANBY TO BYERS CANYON

(See map, page 35.)

Downstream from Lake Granby the Colorado meanders across an outwash plain—the rubble left behind when glaciers retreated as they melted. The broad valley is ranchland, meaning it's privately owned.

Willow Creek is the first significant tributary stream to flow into the Colorado after it leaves Lake Granby. State Highway 125 crosses the stream 5 miles north of U.S. 40. It follows Highway 125 from its head a half-mile south of Willow Creek Pass. It's a small stream, 20 to 30 feet in width. It gets stocked with brookies and rainbows, so it's primarily put-and-take fishing. Willow Creek isn't a destination stream, but if you're passing by and have the time, it's probably worth stopping to wet a line. The upper sections with the beaver ponds, near the pass, look the best.

One mile west of U.S. 34 the Colorado runs beneath U.S. 40. From here, the highway closely follows the course of the stream as it flows westward. The Fraser joins the Colorado here, the confluence being a short distance above the inlet of Windy Gap Reservoir.

The Windy Gap Project is a transmountain water diversion that began operation in 1985. The reservoir is owned and operated by the Northern Colorado Water Conservancy District Municipal Subdistrict. Windy Gap directs water diverted from the Colorado and Fraser Rivers in Grand County to five northeastern Colorado cities: Estes Park, Boulder, Loveland, Longmont, and Greeley, and also to the Platte River Power Authority. Windy Gap water is delivered through the Continental Divide using the physical facilities of the U.S. Bureau of Reclamation's Colorado–Big Thompson Project.

The reservoir is not open to the public for recreation, either for hunting or fishing. It is, however, a wildlife preserve. Duck nesting boxes are placed in the shallow areas of the lake. Geese use the area too. Wildlife observation sites and picnic tables are the only facilities available to the public and are located along the south side of U.S. 40.

Downstream from Windy Gap the river continues its meandering path through Middle Park's ranchland. This marks the beginning of the river's Gold Medal section that extends west to Troublesome Creek. Public access to the Colorado between Windy Gap and Hot Sulphur Springs is virtually nonexistent. At Windy Gap, a mile and a quarter west of State Highway 125, a short stretch of river is accessible from the highway. CDOW signs mark the area, and parking is available off the south shoulder of U.S. 40.

West of Windy Gap the BLM manages the public land along the south side of the Colorado River. Nearly a mile of river here is on public land. But because there are no public roads that give access to the BLM land, anglers are shut out of the property. This is one of many areas within the state in which BLM land benefits agricultural-property owners.

The next public access is at the town of Hot Sulphur Springs. By this point the river has collected the flows of a dozen or so small streams, each of which contributes little, but collectively the volume is significant. One of these small streams is Kinney Creek, which enters the Colorado 3 miles west of Windy Gap. Kinney Creek is designated as a Colorado River cutthroat (a threatened species) recovery stream.

Two miles east of Hot Sulphur Springs the highway crosses the river. This section, from U.S. 40 downstream to Prospect Park, is leased by Rocky Mountain Angling Club, which provides access to members. The club's lease ends at the ranch boundary about a mile north of town. From here downstream to the west end of Hot Sulphur State Wildlife Area the river is open to the public. A fair dirt road runs along the river, following it upstream in Pioneer Park. The road has pullouts along the way, making it easy to get to the stream to fish. Camping is permitted here in the park. Although this area receives a lot of use, the fishing is very good.

Toward the upper end of the public section in Prospect Park, side channels present interesting situations. Brush usually restricts casts to dapping or flipping a short length of line upstream. In spring spawning seasons these small trickles harbor rainbows and browns. Rainbows are here in spring to reproduce. The browns follow, seeking a meal of fresh roe. Egg patterns are your best choice at this season.

Across from the county maintenance shops in Hot Sulphur Springs, a low rock spillway forms a broad, slow pool. The far bank near the shops is a place you'll enjoy drifting a dry fly down the feeding lanes. Long casts are often the rule here until late-season flows allow a closer approach. Even though this part of the river is open to all angling methods, even the use of bait, fly casters will seldom have competition from worm dunkers for this hole.

A few yards downstream from the spillway, a low-sagging power line crosses the river. I speak from experience when I pass on the warning that it is all too easy to snag a backcast on it. Try to keep your fly low as you work a nymph in the lanes here.

Because this part of the river has no special regulations, it gets a lot of pressure. Summer weekends bring out the crowds. Many anglers bring their families to soak up the sun or enjoy a picnic lunch. You'll see Dad or Mom assisting a child, giving him or her a chance to catch the first trout. Sure they use bait, but it is legal here. It's a different river during the week, however. That's when you will want to fish it.

The terrain through Middle Park is a broad, gently sloping valley. Elevation at Windy Gap and Smith Creek is a smidgen under 7,800 feet. Seven miles downstream, at the west end of

Byers Canyon, the river has descended only 350 feet. The land is agricultural, and these ranchers produce hay, their fields irrigated by the river. Along the valley you'll see outcrops of dark-colored rock, the remnants of the volcanism that occurred here a few million years ago. Quite a few small creeks enter the Colorado from the north in the area.

Whirling disease is suspected of causing the disappearance of immature rainbows in the Middle Park section of the Colorado River. Although by itself whirling disease is seldom severely devastating, when other stress-inducing conditions exist the combined effect is to cause high mortality in susceptible trout populations. Other negative conditions on the Colorado include nitrogen supersaturation and low flows over a several-year period. Although CDOW biologists determined in 1994 that four year-classes of rainbow young were not present in the river, the situation is not as bad as many alarmists would have us believe.

The disease has also affected the brown trout population in Middle Park, though to a lesser degree. In their 1994 study of whirling disease, biologists Barry Nehring and Pete Walker also found that cutthroats, though susceptible, were less affected by the disease than were rainbows. The biomass of the river is relatively constant, meaning the rainbows still there are large.

In April 1995 a project was begun to ensure the future of quality angling in Middle Park. CDOW biologists collected 300,000 rainbow eggs with the help of the Rocky Mountain Angling Club and volunteer workers. The eggs were spawned in the Glenwood Springs hatchery and the fry were raised to a size at which the young trout could resist whirling disease. Then the fry were returned to the Colorado.

Though the loss of wild trout is disturbing, anglers must remember that rainbows, browns, and rainbow-cutthroat hybrids are not native to the Colorado River. Rainbows and browns were stocked in the past to establish them. Until a way to eradicate whirling disease is found and other problems are solved, artificially rearing the Colorado River strain of rainbows is one way to preserve the species. It's either that or have no rainbow fishery in Middle Park.

There are no restrictive regulations on this stretch, and anglers are permitted to keep a normal limit of trout. Fishing with flies, lures, and bait is allowed. CDOW is the only government agency controlling regulations on the public sections.

The Rocky Mountain Angling Club controls access and angling methods on their lease upstream from Hot Sulphur Springs.

Windy Gap

This quarter-mile stretch is a broad riffle and a side channel. The area is posted with a CDOW sign listing fishing regulations. The river bottom is littered with large boulders. Both banks are lined with trees and brush. The Grand County Road 57 bridge marks the downstream limit of public access.

➤ Access and Parking

Park on the south side of U.S. 40 east of Grand County Road 57. A footpath leads through the shallow slough by the road to the main channel.

➤ Seasons

The river is first fishable in spring by early April until runoff begins. After the high-water season ends there is good fishing through late fall.

➤ Equipment

Chest waders and a 4-weight rod will do fine.

⌐ Patterns

Dry Flies: Baetis Blue-Winged Olive, Pale Morning Dun, Elkhair Caddis, Humpy, Sofa Pillow, Griffith Gnat, Royal Wulff, Adams, Irresistible, ant, hopper. Nymphs: Halfback, Prince, Twenty-Incher, Gold-Ribbed Hare's Ear, Pheasant Tail, scuds, San Juan Worm (all colors), caddis larvae, egg fly. Emergers: RS-2, Serendipity, Gold-Ribbed Hare's Ear. Streamers: Muddler Minnow, Woolly Bugger.

Pioneer Park

Above Hot Sulphur Springs the river is a gently flowing stream. It is quite broad, exceeding 100 feet. Except during runoff, when an angler who ventures into the current is risking life and rod, it's not difficult to wade. The river bottom consists of a large number of cobbles and boulders that are moderately slick. If one exercises reasonable caution they won't usually present a problem. Felt soles or some other skid-resistant material is advised for your wading shoes. When the flows are up, a wading staff can help you maintain your balance in the faster sections.

Pioneer Park, the public section of this stretch, begins downstream from the private land with a long shallow riffle and continues to the west side of town at Byers Canyon. The current is fast because the gradient is significant. This is good nymphing water, but you'll want to use a minimum amount of weight to prevent snagging the bottom excessively.

After about 300 yards of broad riffles the river becomes deeper and slower. The right bank—the cut bank—is deep. Except late in the summer this side will be tough to wade due to its depth. By making long casts, though, from either bank, you'll be able to drift a nymph or streamer down the middle among the gigantic boulders that offer cover for the fish. The river alternates between deep slow sections and shallow broad riffles down to the entrance to Byers Canyon.

The section through town, both upstream and downstream from the bridge (one block north of U.S. 40) is broad, shallow, and easy to wade in. It is also located conveniently near the campground.

This part of the river muddies fast after thundershowers. When that occurs, try a brown or orange San Juan Worm.

➤ Access and Parking

At Hot Sulphur Springs, turn north at the west end of town. Cross the river at the bridge. Go right on a fair dirt road that follows the river upstream. Parking is available in the campground and at pullouts along the road.

➤ Seasons

The ice usually comes off by early April. Rainbows begin spawning shortly after ice-out. Mid- to late May brings high water, and even though the fishing can be good, when flows exceed 600 cfs wading will be difficult to hazardous. Try fishing the edges along the banks and side channels.

Summer brings lower flows around late June to early July, depending on the amount of snow in the high country. During a normal year this section can be waded with little difficulty in early summer. The Colorado warms quickly in the hot afternoon sun; as on other sections of the river, angling will be best early and late in the day. Fly fishermen will enjoy the mayfly and caddis hatches that occur following runoff.

Fall's cooler temperatures slow the fishing by September and October. Most action comes during the middle of the day, when the air is warmer. There will probably be some midge activity and a few *Baetis* out for some fall dry-fly angling.

➤ Equipment

The rocky bottom tends to be a bit slick, so felt soles will help prevent too many spills. When the water is high, use a wading staff, particularly when the river is colored, for you won't be able to see the bottom very easily. If your favorite rod is a 4-weight, it will be perfect here for all seasons.

➤ Patterns

Stonefly nymphs usually are the best producers after ice-out. Large sizes, about 8–12, work well. When the rainbows begin spawning, egg patterns will take both rainbows and browns. Fish them over the shallow gravel bars. Be careful to avoid disturbing the fish, though: Don't walk through the redds, and stay a reasonable distance from active spawners.

In summer during the middle of the day try stonefly nymphs in the faster water and deep runs. After a rain, a San Juan Worm can be good in the same places. Late afternoon often brings out a few hatches in the shallow pools and back currents. Tie on a small BWO or other *Baetis* pattern. An Elkhair Caddis or Humpy will work for times when larger insects are on the water.

Fall fishing slows down but can be productive during the warmer periods of the day. Small *Baetis* imitations can be good producers then. Dry flies: *Baetis* imitations, Blue-Winged Olive, Pale Morning Dun, Elkhair Caddis, Humpy, Sofa Pillow, Griffith Gnat, Royal Wulff, Adams, Irresistible, ant, hopper. Nymphs: Halfback, Prince, Twenty-Incher, Gold-Ribbed Hare's Ear, Pheasant Tail, scuds, San Juan Worm (all colors), caddis larvae, egg fly. Emergers: RS-2, Serendipity, Gold-Ribbed Hare's Ear. Streamers: Muddler Minnow, Woolly Bugger.

Byers Canyon

This is a narrow steep-sided canyon cut into colorful granite. The river is steep with many short plunges. Although the river is beside U.S. 40, this section is seldom fished because the nearly vertical 100-foot descent appears too intimidating. Downstream from Pioneer Park the river becomes deep. Only the run immediately above the canyon is wadable. In less than 3 miles the river drops 200 feet. The current is strong and the channel narrow, forcing the water to increase velocity. Through the canyon you'll find it safest to fish from the bank. Take care though, because the banks are composed of large boulders and the footing is not always secure. Except during low flows, crossing the river is not advised. Even then, use caution and cross only in the shallow areas.

➤ Access and Parking

From Pioneer Park, walk downstream. The Southern Pacific Railroad owns the right-of-way through Byers Canyon along the Colorado's right bank, which means this area is private property. Even so, many anglers reach the river by walking along the tracks. If you are among them, be careful: trains pass here several times each day.

In the canyon, several parking places are available along U.S. 40, from which you can make your way—carefully—down the boulder-strewn sides. Heed the posted restrictions, for rockfalls are not uncommon, particularly after heavy rains following the spring thaw. At the west end of the canyon use the broad parking area along the north side of U.S. 40. Follow the foot trails along the rubble upstream on the left bank.

➤ Seasons

The canyon section is usually open in April, offering a few weeks of prerunoff angling. Once the snow begins to melt, this

Byers Canyon has some tackle-busting sections.

stretch is going to run too fast to allow fishing with anything lighter than a winch cable for a leader.

Flows won't settle down too much here until late summer because of the restricted width of the canyon. Even when the water *is* low, you won't find a large amount of surface feeding. In some of the deep slow-moving pools, however, fish will take bugs off the top late in the day. Since the canyon makes the descent to the river appear more difficult than it really is, you should have these pools to yourself.

Fall fishing will be similar to fishing in summer, though the air and water will be cooler. This could be an opportunity to hook into fish that are gorging on larger nymphs in preparation for winter.

~ Equipment

Whatever your favorite rod is will work fine here. Because the fish can be large and the current strong, you will want to go with a 3- or 4X tippet. If that proves too light, put on a heavier tippet. The fish won't be too leadershy in this boisterous section.

➤ Patterns

Even when it's running low, this is big water, suggesting the use of large flies. Try some large stonefly patterns (anything with peacock herl) and streamers. Woolly Buggers tied with Krystal Hair have some flash that make them more visible and attractive. At either end of the canyon you will find some good dry-fly fishing. Use midge imitations, BWOs, and caddis patterns.

Dry flies: Baetis, Blue-Winged Olive, Pale Morning Dun, Elkhair Caddis, Humpy, Sofa Pillow, Griffith Gnat, Royal Wulff, Adams, Irresistible, ant, hopper. Nymphs: Halfback, Prince, Twenty-Incher, Gold-Ribbed Hare's Ear, Pheasant Tail, scuds, San Juan Worm (all colors), caddis larvae, egg fly. Emergers: RS-2, Serendipity, Gold-Ribbed Hare's Ear. Streamers: Muddler Minnow, Woolly Bugger.

The Colorado has been good to me. Through Middle Park it has rewarded me with fish every time I've tossed a fly on the surface or dredged a nymph along the bottom. It's a part of the river I have named Old Faithful because it always provides action.

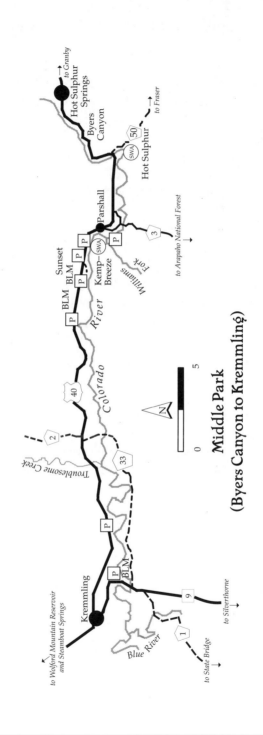

Middle Park
(Byers Canyon to Kremmling)

to Granby

Hot Sulphur
Springs

Byers
Canyon

to Fraser

50

SWA

Hot Sulphur

Parshall

Sunset

BLM

BLM

BLM

P

P

P

P

P

Kemp-
Breeze

SWA

P

3

to Arapaho National Forest

Williams Fork

River

Colorado

40

2

Troublesome Creek

33

P

P

BLM

Kremmling

to Wolford Mountain Reservoir
and Steamboat Springs

9

to Silverthorne

1

Blue River

to State Bridge

N

0   5

MIDDLE PARK: BYERS CANYON TO KREMMLING

West of Byers Canyon, almost half the river is open to all anglers: The Bureau of Land Management has property here that is open to the public, and CDOW has added to the inventory of fishing access too.

After leaving Byers Canyon the river regains the docile nature it will retain over much of its length through Middle Park. In the section between the canyon and Kremmling the Colorado meanders on its way toward Gore Canyon. The Valley of the Grand is small as such parks go. Both North Park, the basin drained by the North Platte River, and South Park, known for the South Platte River and Spinney Mountain Reservoir, are miles across.

Middle Park is often little more than a half-mile in breadth. Former point bars, areas filled with coarse rock as the channel worked its way across the valley, are now hay meadows. The current course of the river is lower, having scoured into ancient sediments and granites. As would be expected, the river's bottom is rocky and made up of an assortment of sand, pebbles, cobbles, and boulders. Not surprisingly, the larger rocks create the majority of fish-holding structures in this part of the Colorado. The rocks are slippery—take it easy when wading.

The river spreads out after exiting Byers Canyon, exceeding 100 feet in width in many places. The gradient is low except in a few spots, and the river is quite broad, therefore shallow. Wading isn't normally difficult, though there are a few exceptions: slippery rocks, holes below drop structures, bridges, and runoff. Trees and brush line much of both banks, serving to make both ingress and egress a challenge and to provide bankside cover for trout. In spite of the brush, access to the water is not terribly difficult.

At a number of sites the stream divides into multiple channels, both naturally and due to irrigation diversions. Don't pass by any such side channels, for even small ones can have fish, especially during spawning periods.

Elevation through this part of Middle Park runs from 7,600 feet at the west end of Byers Canyon to a bit over 7,200 feet south of Kremmling.

Between Byers Canyon and the confluence of Troublesome Creek east of Kremmling, CDOW manages the river downstream as Wild Trout and Gold Medal Water. Fishing methods are restricted to flies and lures only.

The Colorado Division of Wildlife reviews fishing and hunting regulations every five years and seeks public input for revisions. In early 1992, petitions began showing up in fly shops for anglers' signatures, requesting that CDOW manage the Colorado in Middle Park as catch-and-release, as it does a few other rivers in the state. To make a long story short, the petitioners prevailed, and since January 1, 1993 the section downstream from Byers Canyon to Troublesome Creek has been managed as a catch-and-release fishery. Although it's not required, many anglers on this stretch choose to use barbless hooks or to pinch down the barbs, reducing the probability of mortally injuring a fish.

Hot Sulphur State Wildlife Area

At the west end of Byers Canyon the Hot Sulphur State Wildlife Area provides public access to about 2 miles of the river. The Wildlife Area's boundary begins in Byers Canyon a quarter-mile upstream from the highway bridge.

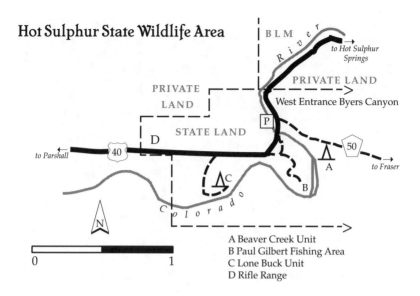

Hot Sulphur State Wildlife Area

BLM

River

to Hot Sulphur Springs

PRIVATE LAND

PRIVATE LAND ->
West Entrance Byers Canyon

P

STATE LAND

D

40

to Parshall

50

A

to Fraser

C

B

Colorado

N

0   1

A Beaver Creek Unit
B Paul Gilbert Fishing Area
C Lone Buck Unit
D Rifle Range

At the west end of the bridge, go south on Grand County Road 50 a few feet to the Paul Gilbert Fishing Area and Beaver Creek Unit. A crude dirt road takes you to the river and unimproved campsites along the left (east) bank of the Colorado. To reach the river here, you will have to force your way through the dense streamside brush.

The Highway 40 bridge constricts the channel, deepening it and accelerating the current. Once past this narrowed section, the river spreads out in excess of 100 feet. It becomes relatively shallow and easier to wade during normal flows (100–300 cfs). The bottom is covered with sediment varying in size from coarse sand to pebbles (up to 2-inch-diameter), cobbles (2- to 10-inch diameter), and boulders (greater than 10-inch-diameter). Although the surface appears rather uniform, variations in the bottom produce fish habitat. Boulders are the most obvious features, but a look below the surface (you *are* wearing polarized glasses, aren't you?) reveals holes and channels that create fish-holding water.

An angler tests the water in the Paul Gilbert Fishing Area.

The Paul Gilbert Fishing area extends downstream from the Highway 40 bridge for about $1^1/_2$ miles of stream. The next access point is immediately past the west end of the bridge. Turn left on the dirt road leading past the Division of Wildlife buildings and follow the road down the hill to the river. Park among the trees on the point bar near the river. Camping is not permitted here, but the area has picnic tables and chemical toilets. Although there are no handicapped facilities such as ramps, the right bank with its easy slope and shallow flow will make wheelchair access along the river possible.

In this area the river again broadens after being squeezed and divided into multiple channels. Willows line the right bank but are not so dense as to make river access difficult. The left bank is steep and high, covered with brush and trees. The current, on the outside bend, more effectively erodes the left bank, deepening the channel. Overhanging branches and the deeper water shelter the fish most of the day.

One-half mile west of the highway bridge, another road leads south, at first across the old terrace, then down to the river on the Lone Buck Unit. The crude path runs parallel to the river for about 300 yards. Facilities in the parking area are limited to chemical toilets, and camping is allowed.

The Paul Gilbert Fishing Unit below the CDOW maintenance yard attracts wildlife. When you sit down at a picnic table, ground squirrels will beg for handouts. One August day anglers were entertained by a family of mink scurrying among the tree roots on the far bank. Deer, elk, and antelope inhabit the region. Often anglers will scare up ducks from the river.

There is a CDOW public rifle and pistol range to the north across U.S. 40 from the Lone Buck Unit. A good dirt road provides access to shooting benches. Bring your own targets. There is no charge to use the range.

➤ Access and Parking

The Beaver Creek Unit is at the west end of Byers Canyon. At the east end of the Highway 40 bridge go south on Grand County Road 50. Parking and campsites are on the left (east) side of the river.

The Paul Gilbert Unit is reached from the west end of the bridge. Go south on the road to the CDOW buildings, then down the hill to the parking area on the north side of the river. Camping is not permitted here, but there are picnic tables and toilets.

The Lone Buck Unit is located one-half mile west of the U.S. 40 bridge and to the south. Camping is allowed here along the north side of the river.

➤ Seasons

The river is seldom free of ice before late March. As is true of high lakes, ice-out is a prime time on the Colorado. The warming water stirs the trouts' appetites. A lack of abundant hatches means you'll want to use nymphs. The river here is full of bug life and is known for its stoneflies. As soon as the rainbows begin spawning you'll be able to take rainbows and browns. You'll often find the fish tight against the bank in water too shallow to cover their fins. Fish the small side channels, even if they appear too shallow for a fish to swim there. Be careful though to avoid disturbing the spawners. Because the rainbows have had poor spawning success in recent years, consider fishing other sections of the river during spawning, or concentrate on the browns.

Although there's not a lot of surface activity this early in the spring, warmer parts of the day may induce a hatch. Action may not be fast, but it will give you a chance to work out the kinks in your dry-fly presentation.

What's amazing about the Colorado through Middle Park is how well it fishes through the runoff. Even at a flow of 600 cfs and in water that resembles chocolate milk, it's possible to have a productive day. Success, naturally, depends on adapting tactics to conditions. With high and dirty water you'll want to be careful where you wade if you venture far from the bank. The current's strength and the water's depth create treacherous conditions. Getting out far, even if it's easy, isn't necessary. Long casts aren't needed because the fish will usually be in close to the banks. Work a peacock-herl-body nymph against the bank and out into the faster current. Be a bit more patient when the water's high and dirty, because the fish will have more difficulty finding your offering. If you do wade, use caution, for the current is quite strong.

Middle Park is ranch country, and many of the ancient river terraces are used to raise hay. The fields are irrigated, and standing water makes a great mosquito hatchery. Don't forget your insect repellent.

The beginning of summer normally corresponds with the tail end of runoff. Because the Colorado through Middle Park is not a tailwater, its temperatures vary throughout the day. This becomes more noticeable as flows drop below 150 cfs. The river has quite a few slow shallow runs that are exposed to the sun at this time of year.

You'll find the fish more active early in the morning and during cooler times of the day. Anglers who get on the river shortly after sunup do best. Often the morning feeding period is finished as early as 8:00 A.M., though it may sometimes last until 10 or so. Weather, of course, also influences day-to-day variations in conditions. The few very hot days of August make for even shorter prime times, and they will be early and late in the day. Overcast days and cool temperatures can have the opposite effect. A front producing thunderstorms may dirty the water for a brief period.

Then there are times when you should ignore all the rules. These are the rare occasions when everything comes together for those who are on the river at the right time. First you notice a tiny dark mayfly drifting in a narrow fast current. A flash of color and a swirl get your attention as the tiny *Baetis* is engulfed in the jaws of a brown so large your legs tremble from seeing it. A few minutes later insects are everywhere on the water and the browns are enjoying a frenzy of feeding. Sometimes these periods are brief, finished by the time you have changed your fly. Usually, though, you can get in a good hour or more of dry-fly action. Watch for such flurries of activity in midafternoon, after the sun is no longer directly hitting the runs beneath the shaded south banks.

Fall brings change to the Colorado. The air begins to cool, the sky darkens to a deep azure contrasting with the thin white cirrus clouds that herald coming snow. September brings the season's first serious frost. This in turn induces changes in streamside trees and brush. Greens fade, replaced by yellows, reds, and oranges as the foliage adorns itself in its finest autumn splendor. In the river, trout sense the coming winter and feed with abandon in preparation for a season of cold and famine. In spite of their hunger, food is now scarce for them. Insects are few, and those that do appear are small, hardly more than a taste.

The changing season brings an alteration in a trout's feeding behavior. Water temperatures drop, and it takes longer for the river to warm sufficiently to induce a midge or *Baetis* hatch at midday. Long afternoon shadows cool the water earlier. The trout have less time for feeding. What this means to the angler is that it's no longer necessary to get on the river at dawn. We can sleep in and still enjoy pleasant fishing. Remember, too, that small-game seasons open on September 1. After taking a couple of blue grouse in the nearby national forest, you can stop off on the Colorado during the middle of the day.

October and November bring even more restricted angling hours. By midautumn the fish may not be seriously active until after noon. Though a few midges may be out during the warmest hours, the trout will be most interested in nymphs. By November the water temperature hovers a bit above freezing and the trout are more lethargic. In spite of a few warm days the ice on the banks slowly begins to creep across the river, closing the channel.

⬥ Equipment

Having a width often exceeding 100 feet and many deep holes, the Colorado between Granby and Kremmling is a major stream. As such, it is difficult to fish with hip waders. Chest waders are necessary, but during July and August water temperatures in the sixties make lightweights comfortable.

Though it's not as slick as some rivers, the footing here can be tricky in the strong currents. A wading staff gives anglers a handy third leg for difficult conditions.

As for rods, the lightest that still allows long—30–50 feet—casts will work fine. Because the fish run from a half-pound on up to several pounds in size, your reel becomes more important here. You'll find it necessary to frequently play the fish from the reel rather than to hand-strip line. Any single-action model with a smooth drag will suffice.

➤ Patterns

The best early-season nymph patterns include the Halfback, Twenty-Incher, Prince, and anything else that's large and tied with peacock herl. Even though the stones grow quite large here, #8–12 nymphs seem to work best. Rig up with the usual nymph arrangement—a small bit of soft lead 1 to 2 feet from the fly, and a strike indicator. Use heavy tippets for this rig, 3X or 4X. The fish aren't leadershy at this time. Fish stonefly patterns in the deeper parts of channels.

Almost as soon as the river opens, the rainbows go into a spawning mode. That's when trout become suckers for egg patterns. The usual colors—salmon, pink, red—work well.

Something that happens on the Colorado beginning in late May is the stonefly, or willow fly, hatch. Those big black nymphs begin to crawl out from beneath the rocks and shed their cases. Montana has nothing on the Colorado River during this emergence. The bugs are large, as big as a small airplane. They make a mouthwatering, stomach-filling meal for even the largest hungry binge-crazed trout. Since the hatch usually peaks during the runoff, you can make good use of a large heavy rod, say an 8-weight. The high water will make long casts essential, and a heavy rod will do the job with ease and impart less strain on your back and shoulders.

One thing to keep in mind is that the fish will stay attuned to these large insects for some time past the hatch. Even if you don't find adult stones on the water, cast a #6 Sofa Pillow beneath the brush along a bank and hang on. With patience, and using proper tactics for the conditions, you can enjoy good fishing during an otherwise difficult period.

As soon as the runoff is done, usually by early July or even late June, Elkhair Caddises make good searching patterns, as do Humpys. Trout are still thinking big, because willow flies have been imprinted on their brains. Warming water temperatures step up trout metabolism. A large fly looks appetizing, say a #12 or #14 of either pattern.

Summer days are also good times to tie on a terrestrial pattern. Ants are attractive even when nothing is hatching. On an August afternoon, Jean—Mrs. Marlowe—embarrassed two male anglers who will remain nameless (but one of whom is her husband) by using a black ant, a fly we men knew wouldn't catch a fish on the Colorado.

Dry flies: *Baetis* imitations, Blue-Winged Olive, Pale Morning Dun, Elkhair Caddis, Humpy, Sofa Pillow, Griffith Gnat, Royal Wulff, Adams, Irresistible, ant, hopper. Nymphs: Halfback, Prince, Twenty-Incher, Gold-Ribbed Hare's Ear, Pheasant Tail, scuds, San Juan Worm, caddis larvae, egg fly. Emergers: RS-2, Serendipity, Gold-Ribbed Hare's Ear with Flashback wingcase. Streamers: Muddler Minnow, Woolly Bugger, Hornberg.

Kemp-Breeze State Wildlife Area

This property provides access to about 3 miles of the Colorado and the Williams Fork downstream from Williams Fork Reservoir and the confluence. Kemp-Breeze has three access points. The first, the Kemp Unit, is off Grand County Road 3, south from U.S. 40 at the east end of Parshall. The county road eventually leads to the headwaters of the Williams Fork. The access area is marked with a large CDOW sign with a map of the area. From the parking lot, access to either river is by foot trail, about a mile's walk to the confluence.

In 1993, following several delays and false starts—a situation similar to the announced opening of Denver International Airport—the Kemp-Breeze property was opened for fishing. Until CDOW acquired this property, the old Corral Creek Ranch had been

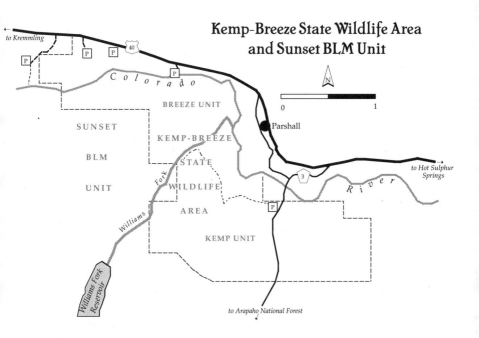

Kemp-Breeze State Wildlife Area and Sunset BLM Unit

off-limits to anglers. The Denver Water Board obtained the ranch, anticipating future water needs and transfers when Two Forks Dam would be built on the South Platte River south of Denver. When the Environmental Protection Agency denied the water board's permit for Two Forks, the ranch was no longer needed. CDOW saw an opportunity, and now this property is one of many tracts throughout Colorado the agency has procured for hunters and anglers.

Remember that just as the river changes its course over time, land ownership changes too. State and federal agencies dispose of and acquire new property. Land trades are common with the USFS and BLM. Isolated tracts are sometimes swapped for other desirable land, opening access to properties long closed to the public. The Kemp-Breeze purchase is only the most recent of such transfers. Other deals will undoubtedly occur in the future. Perhaps the next acquisition will open a section of the river you've long wanted to fish.

The character of the river here is much the same as on other sections in Middle Park below Byers Canyon. The river is a freestone stream. The bottom is covered with boulders. The rocks have a thin coating of moss that makes footing interesting, especially when the flows are up. The river is large, too. It doesn't compare to the Mississippi, but for a section so near its headwaters, the size of the river here is significant. There is an incredible amount of fishable water, and it isn't necessary to cover a great length of the river to find fish.

After picking up the Williams Fork, the Colorado's volume of water can more than double. The riffle sections are worth spending time fishing. Unlike those of a small creek, these riffles can be 2 and 3 feet deep. And although the water's surface may appear featureless, a look beneath shows, to paraphrase Carl Sagan, "millions and millions" of structures to hold fish. During summer hatches, early morning and mid- to late afternoon will find fish surface feeding. At other times, try drifting a #8 Halfback or a Gold-Ribbed Hare's Ear weighted to get it down near and just above the bottom. With so much water, it's going to take time to work it properly and thoroughly. With this latest addition to the inventory of public land on the Colorado, between Granby and Kremmling one can fish roughly 9 or 10 miles of the river. By fishing slowly and methodically, this section alone could take you all summer and most of the fall.

Following the purchase of the Kemp-Breeze property, anglers not only have new access to a long stretch of the Colorado but we also picked up nearly a mile of the Williams Fork. The Fork is perhaps half the width of the river it joins, though its flow is significant. During runoff, it can add 1,000 cfs to the Colorado.

This mile of river is fast water with small holding pools—pocket water. Because of this, the river fishes well with nymphs. Dana Rikimaru, an Orvis School fly fishing instructor with The Blue Quill Angler in Evergreen, says the Williams Fork fishes well with stonefly imitations, Gold-Ribbed Hare's Ears, and Pheasant

An angler fishes the Breeze property.

Tails. An enthusiastic angler, she also says that small caddis are in the river and are worth trying in July and August. The river has rainbows, but most of your catch will be browns, and they can run to 3 or 4 pounds. It appears that CDOW did well in adding this property to the angler's inventory.

Like the Colorado, the bottom of the Williams Fork is covered primarily with large rocks. Felt soles should be adequate to prevent slipping too much. With the fast current, though, you may want to use a wading staff.

Cutbanks can present an interesting problem. In a few places the river's current energy has cut deep into the banks, creating holes that a big brown will head to for safety after being hooked. Such holes are often repositories for natural litter—overhanging brush, driftwood, and other material carried by the current. Debris that protects the fish will also foul light tippets, enabling fish to escape. There's nothing we can do about this condition other than be aware of it.

The only access to this part of the Williams Fork is from the parking lot at the Kemp Unit. A three-quarter-mile trail leads to the water. Be careful where you step because there's a considerable amount of barbed wire lying about from the ranch that previously occupied this property. It can not only trip you but may also tear holes in your expensive neoprene waders.

Moving upstream from Williams Fork Reservoir the river is a beautiful high-mountain stream. It heads below peaks of the Williams Fork and Vasquez mountains to the south. Most of its 25 miles is within the Arapaho National Forest, which means public access. Campgrounds provide a base for fishing the Williams Fork and the Colorado.

~ Access and Parking

The Kemp Unit is located 2 miles west of Byers Canyon and 12 miles east of Kremmling. Take Grand County Road 3 south across the river 0.3-mile to the parking area marked with a CDOW sign.

The Breeze Unit parking lot is located along U.S. 40 a mile west of Parshall. The exit from the highway is marked with a sign reading "Fishing Access." Follow the gravel path a couple hundred yards to the parking area that is situated on a gravel terrace marking a former level of the river. From here, follow footpaths leading down the terrace to the river.

Additional access to the Breeze Unit is located about one-half mile farther west. The river is only a few feet from U.S. 40 between these two parking lots, and many anglers choose to stop along the shoulder, which does have trees, providing a shaded stopping place.

➤ Seasons

The Williams Fork below Williams Fork Reservoir has sufficiently warm water to stay open, and as a result, the Colorado is open for a short distance in the Breeze Unit. Other than for being open in winter, when fishing success is primarily with small—#20 and smaller—patterns, conditions throughout the year are the same as those previously described on pages 55–58.

West of Parshall, a few sections are seldom shut down. The quarter-mile-long Parshall BLM run is one of these places. They frequently run slush ice, though, and the water temperatures are low enough to inhibit any serious feeding activity.

➤ Equipment

Middle Park can get cold in winter. Those who fish often in below-freezing weather may find the conditions tough on fly lines. The plastic finish can become brittle and break, leaving only the core intact. For such severe conditions, some anglers are loading their reel with 40-pound squidding line, which is unaffected by the cold. Since winter fishing here is short-line nymphing, a bit of weight on the leader is sufficient for casting.

Equipment recommendations are the same as described on pages 55–60.

➤ Patterns
Suggested patterns are listed on pages 59–60.

Sunset BLM Unit
(See map, page 61.)

The Sunset BLM property is located west of and adjoins the Kemp-Breeze property. The parking lot is a mile west of the Breeze Unit's west boundary. A sign marks the access road, which crosses private land. You will park on a terrace above the river. Follow a footpath south a half-mile to the river. The path is a road that is now closed to vehicles. The trail descends a steep slope consisting of eroded shales. It gets muddy and slippery when wet. Use caution here during thunderstorms, for the area is exposed. The only protection from lightning is a barbed-wire fence beside the parking lot.

This stretch is among the most pleasant on the Colorado. The river flows nearly in a straight line through the Sunset Unit. It is broad and shallow. The rocky bottom makes this a long riffle, and there are a few large boulders in the river creating obvious structures. The subtle structures, though, are those smaller rocks creating this massive riffle. Brush along the banks rarely intrudes on the channel, so casting is no problem. To properly fish this mile of water could require a full day.

The stretch of river that begins in a lazy fashion changes abruptly at the west end of the Sunset Unit. For the last few yards the river becomes deeper and faster. This is one of Murphy's

The Sunset BLM section adjoins the Kemp-Breeze property.

favorite sections. He says the deep hole at the west end of the property beneath a decrepit rustic bridge is home to a 24-inch rainbow he has seen many times. If Murphy reads this and sees that I've given away one of his secrets, I'm in deep trouble— deeper than the rainbow's resting place.

A quarter-mile stretch of river on BLM property is accessible a mile west of the Sunset Unit and on the south side of U.S. 40. Parking is limited—it's only large enough for two or three cars. To get to the river, cross the fence over a stile. Wire strands across the river mark the east and west boundaries of the BLM section.

➤ Access and Parking

An access road heads south of U.S. 40 2 miles west of Parshall, or 10 miles east of Kremmling. The dirt road ends about a quarter-mile from the highway. From the parking area, walk along the former road south to the river.

⌁ Seasons, Equipment, and Patterns

See listings under the Hot Sulphur State Wildlife Areas,
pages 55–60. This stretch of river is usually covered with ice in
winter.

Troublesome Creek

This small meandering meadow stream joins the Colorado
5 miles east of Kremmling. It is reported to hold some better-than-
average browns. The stream is privately owned with the exception of a half-mile-long stretch on the Troublesome Valley Ranch
Unit, a State Trust Land property. The creek on this property is of
little interest to anglers because it isn't open for public access
until September 1 and the water is too shallow then to provide
cover for fish. Some sections on the lower part of Troublesome
Creek may be open for guided fishing.

Wolford Mountain Reservoir and Muddy Creek

Less than a quarter-mile west of Kremmling, U.S. 40 crosses
a small formerly chocolate-colored stream. Muddy Creek heads
near Rabbit Ears Pass and cuts through a broad valley all the way
to the Colorado River. Wandering over easily eroded shale, Muddy
Creek transports a high volume of suspended sediment. Because
the pastures lining it are used for grazing, Muddy Creek very
likely also carries nitrates, which were dumped into the Colorado
River until 1995.

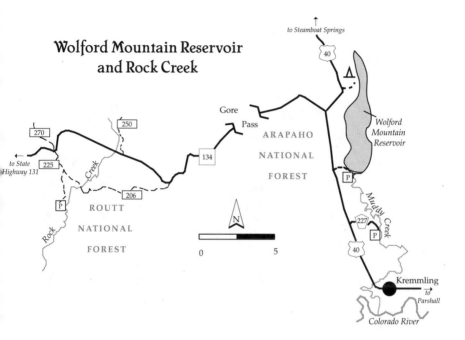

Wolford Mountain Reservoir
and Rock Creek

In 1993, construction began on Wolford Mountain Dam near Kremmling. The reservoir is intended to pay back water diverted by Windy Gap, a small reservoir a mile west of Granby beside U.S. 40. The Northern Colorado Water Conservancy District, which built Windy Gap, was obligated to pay $10.2 million toward the nearly $50 million cost of Wolford Mountain Dam.

Some may recall that in 1987 the water district made public their plans to construct a dam on Rock Creek, a small stream 5 miles west of Gore Pass. The U.S. Forest Service did an environmental impact study and hosted hearings around the state beginning that year. I attended these hearings and wrote letters to the U.S. Forest Service, opposing the Rock Creek dam. The opposition prevailed and the alternate Wolford Mountain site was eventually chosen for the reservoir.

Wolford Mountain Reservoir began filling in 1995 and is expected to have several benefits. First, it will provide a new flat-water

With the completion of Wolford Mountain Dam, Muddy Creek has become clear.

fishery that should be good for the first few years. According to Eddie Kochman, Aquatic Wildlife Manager for the Colorado Division of Wildlife, the reservoir will be managed as a trout fishery even though it is better suited for cool water species. Because of the endangered and threatened species in the Colorado drainage, such as squawfish and suckers, northern pike and walleyes will not be stocked here. Boat ramps and a campground were built at the north end of the reservoir. The water district will assume part of the cost for stocking the new reservoir.

A second plus from the dam is that Muddy Creek's sediment will settle in the impoundment. Clear water will be released below the dam, possibly creating a tailwater fishery. Before this can be realized, however, the tailwater will need some help. The creek channel below the dam is deep and fast with few if any fish-holding structures. If boulders, wing-deflectors, and willows are placed or planted along the banks, Muddy Creek could become a fair fishery. The clear-water releases will benefit the Colorado, too.

The third improvement will benefit the Blue River. Its flows are expected to stabilize because water that is released from Dillon and Green Mountain Reservoirs will be replaced with water from Wolford Mountain Dam.

By the summer of 1996, rainbows, cuttbows, browns, and brooks stocked the year before had grown to lengths of 12 to 14 inches. The Colorado Division of Wildlife added kokanee salmon and Snake River cutthroat fingerlings to the lake in 1996. As with new reservoirs, feed conditions should induce rapid growth for several years. All angling methods are legal here, and a bag of 8 trout is allowed.

➤ Access and Parking

Go 3 miles west from Kremmling on U.S. 40 to the south access road that leads to the dam. Parking and use in this area are free. Limited facilities here include sheltered picnic tables and restrooms. To reach the tailwater, walk east from the parking area down to the creek, about one-quarter mile.

County Road 227, about 2 miles west of Kremmling, accesses Muddy Creek below the reservoir. Because much of it runs through BLM property, which is marked, almost 2 miles of stream is available to anglers.

One mile north of State Highway 134, an access road leads east to the boat ramp and campground. A three-dollar daily use fee is charged for entrance; campsites with electric hookups cost $10 per night. Water is available. RVers will be able to dump their holding tanks at this facility.

➤ Seasons

Muddy Creek, immediately below the reservoir, could possibly have open water most of the year and should run clear. Because

Colorado River Middle Park Hatch Chart: Byers Canyon to Kremmling												
	Jan	Feb	Mar	Apr	May	Jun	Jul	Aug	Sep	Oct	Nov	Dec
Blue-Winged Olive						■	■	■	■	■		
Pale Morning Dun					■	■	■					
Rusty Spinner						■	■	■				
Green Drake							■	■				
Trico								■	■	■		
Tiny Western Olive						■	■	■	■			
Caddis						■	■	■	■			
Stoneflies												
Pteronarcys					■	■						
Golden						■	■					
Ants							■	■	■	■		
Hoppers								■				
Midges				■	■	■	■	■	■	■		

the stream runs through open country with no cover, the lower sections may freeze in winter.

The reservoir should offer year-round recreation for those who enjoy ice fishing. It can provide good waterfowl hunting, too.

The Colorado is not an intimidating river to fish. Unlike fish in rivers such as the South Platte, the fish here haven't yet earned their Ph.D.s in pattern recognition. With the exception of fishing Blue-Winged Olives in August or midges in the fall, minuscule flies are not required. It's a forgiving river enjoyed equally by the expert and the first-time fly fisher.

Keep one thing in mind regarding patterns: Don't limit yourself to any list of flies. While fishing one October and having little success (actually none) on the usual stuff, my friend Dave Haubert caught several nice fish on a—are you paying attention?—tan scud. I had never thought of the Colorado as being a place to fish scuds, having always associated them with tailwaters or lakes and ponds. To make a long story short, I tied one on and caught fish.

It has been a rare day when I've had no action at all on the Colorado. When it did happen, there were usually extenuating circumstances. Some less-than-ideal situations included rare days in early spring when nothing was happening; the water would be cold and the fish asleep. On another day, my only excuse for no hits was the ice that covered the river. The only reason I even went fishing was because several shops assured me that the fishing was great. Guess I should have been there the day before or something like that.

A brown's hunger can set up amusing situations, as it did for me. The water still ran a bit high, around 200 cfs, but it was clear. Standing in the middle of the river, I watched a brown rising in the shallows near the right bank. The fish looked about 16 inches— not huge, but respectable. Though it was midafternoon, the large mayflies resembled PMDs. I cast a large light-colored Humpy above the fish, which rose at regular intervals in one spot. After a few drifts a fish hit and was on but only for a few moments, when my tippet snapped. I repaired my terminal tackle and tied on a new fly to resume fishing. A rise caught my attention. I watched. The rises were in the same spot as before. It looked like a brown of about 16 inches. Has to be the same fish, I thought. Why not get my fly back? I made several casts with the new Humpy, all of which the brown ignored. Would you go back to the same greasy spoon where you got heartburn yesterday? This fish learned from mistakes.

My attempts to hook the fish a second time had not put it down. Since it refused my Humpy, I tried an Elkhair Caddis in the same spot. It worked. The brown hit, and we connected. This is pretty good, I mused, I'll get my Humpy back. It didn't work out, though—Hook slipped out. At least my tippet didn't break. The fish got an education that day, learning two new patterns to avoid in the future.

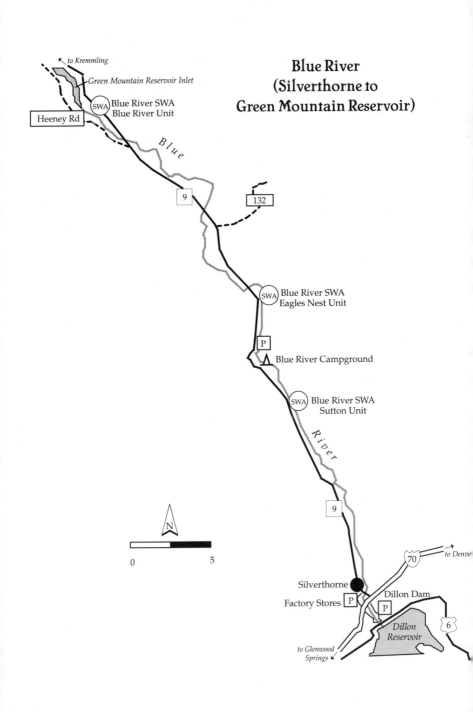

Blue River
(Silverthorne to
Green Mountain Reservoir)

to Kremmling

Green Mountain Reservoir Inlet

Blue River SWA
Blue River Unit

Heeney Rd

Blue

9

132

Blue River SWA
Eagles Nest Unit

P

Blue River Campground

Blue River SWA
Sutton Unit

River

9

N

0   5

70   to Denver

Silverthorne

Factory Stores   P

Dillon Dam

P

Dillon
Reservoir

6

to Glenwood
Springs

BLUE RIVER

The Blue River heads on the north side of Hoosier Pass, about 20 miles south of the town of Dillon. After filling two reservoirs it joins the Colorado at Kremmling. The Colorado Division of Wildlife classifies the river between Dillon Dam and the Colorado River Gold Medal Water, with the exception of Green Mountain Reservoir. The 2.5-mile stretch below Green Mountain Dam is Wild Trout Water.

The Blue receives its name not from the clarity or color of the water but from the native Utes' observation of the country. They called it the "river of the valley of the blue sky."

From its headwaters down to Dillon Reservoir the Blue is a small mountain stream, around 20 feet in width. For most of its length above the reservoir public access is limited because most of the land along the river is privately owned. The collection of small creeks that merge to create the Blue get together above 10,400 feet beside State Highway 9. By the time it pours into Dillon Reservoir the river has plunged more than 1,000 feet to an elevation of 9,025 feet. The river flows through a mineralized region that has produced a wealth of gold from many placer deposits.

Silverthorne

Your best bet for fishing the Blue is likely the tailwater between Dillon Reservoir and the factory outlet stores in Silverthorne. Randy Smith, world-famous fly tier from Breckenridge, Colorado, has confirmed the presence of big rainbows of 9 and 10 pounds. Randy did it the old-fashioned way: He caught them.

Dillon Reservoir has been around since the 1960s, but it's only recently that the tailwater below the reservoir has arrived at its potential. Though this might be considered tinkering with artificial habitat, mysis shrimp were put into the reservoir. Those that make it through the outlet gates provide a trout-style smorgasbord below the dam. Anglers who recall the football-shaped rainbows below Reudi Dam on the Fryingpan in the 1980s know what awaits them now on the Blue.

Past the blacktopped parking lots for the factory stores, man's work restricts the river's ability to behave properly. The outflow from Dillon Dam runs in a canal here rather than a channel. The bottom is covered with cobbles and boulders. As is true of other tailwaters, the Blue at Silverthorne runs clear and cold.

Structures in the river include deep holes, riffles, and large boulders for trout to hide in, under, or behind. Randy says they hide quite well. Their camouflage markings and coloration allow the rainbows to blend with the dark bottom—they tend to be hard to spot. He highly recommends using polarized glasses to locate fish. You may need to get up on the bank to have a better angle for peering into the water. He says it's important to locate the fish because fishing the water is usually unproductive. The situation is exacerbated in winter, when fish are less inclined to move more than a few inches to sample your nymph.

Hits will often be subtle. Your strike indicator may barely move, particularly in cold-water conditions. Randy suggests setting the hook any time the indicator slows its movement or changes direction, even if the movement is no more than a centimeter.

Although rainbows and browns are the most common species here, the tailwater also holds brookies. With plenty of mysis shrimp to feed on, they grow to sizable proportions. Don't be surprised to take one of 18 inches.

Use caution when wading this section. Fast, deep currents and a slick bottom make for slippery wading. Move slowly and make certain one foot is solidly placed before moving the other. A wading staff can help you avoid accidental dunkings.

From Dillon Dam through the town of Silverthorne all trout must be returned to the water immediately and unharmed.

⬤ Access and Parking

Between Dillon Dam and State Highway 9, anglers have more than one-half-mile of river to fish. The factory outlet stores at Silverthorne offer plenty of parking spaces close to the river. Anglers wearing neoprene waders and carrying fly rods are a common sight here. Between the outlet stores and the dam, a road follows the river. Pullouts along the road provide parking close to the water. Immediately below the dam a bridge provides a way to cross the river. No angling is allowed upstream of the bridge.

⬤ Seasons

Because this is a tailwater fishery it is open year-round. Water temperatures in winter typically are low—not much above freezing. Because the Blue is one of the few rivers close to Denver with open water in winter, it can be a busy place on a weekend.

Late spring is about the only time conditions vary significantly due to runoff, at least in average years. Flows generally run anywhere from 50 to 100 cfs through most of the year and peak in spring at around 300 cfs. The river is usually clear below the dam, but during the snowmelt period runoff from Straight and Tenmile Creeks will dirty the water for a while below the stores.

⬤ Equipment

When fishing the factory outlet store section below Dillon Dam, consider the size of the fish. Hogs are not unusual, so don't go too light in selecting a rod. A 4-weight may be as light as should be used here. Since the Blue is not a huge river, long casts are not frequently necessary to reach the far bank. A 4-weight may just be the perfect rod for this river. Consider the larger fish again in selecting a reel. To handle an 8- or 9-pound rainbow you will need one with a good smooth drag.

With a dam controlling its flows, the Blue runs colder than many rivers in the state. Low water temperatures, even through much of the summer, suggest the use of neoprene waders in the tailwater stretches.

Even with usually clear water conditions, fish can be difficult to spot here. Polarized glasses with brown or amber lenses reduce glare and increase contrast, making it easier to find well-camou-flaged fish.

⤙ Patterns

Because of the cold water flowing out of the dam, the insects here tend to be small. Midges and midge larvae are the most commonly used flies in all but the summer months.

Dry flies: Caddis, midges. Nymphs: Caddis larvae, Gold-Ribbed Hare's Ear, Pheasant Tail, midge larvae and emergers (Black Beauty, Black Zing Wing, Biot Midge Pupa), mysis shrimp. Streamers: Woolly Bugger.

Silverthorne to Green Mountain Reservoir

Below the town of Silverthorne the valley's character changes. It broadens, though it's still flanked on the east and west by high ranges with peaks, some exceeding 13,000 feet. Eagles Nest Peak, situated in the Eagles Nest Wilderness Area,

A few isolated stretches of the Blue River are on BLM property.

is a prominent landmark on the west side of the valley. By the time the river flows into Green Mountain Reservoir 18 miles north of Silverthorne, the valley is much broader, its flanks rolling sagebrush-covered slopes dotted with conifers at the higher elevations.

Downstream from Silverthorne the Blue is a multiple-use river and is popular in the summer with rafters. Fishing access is limited because most of the Blue runs through private property. Scattered tracts of Arapaho National Forest land, BLM property, and a State Wildlife Area offer public access on this stretch.

Between Silverthorne and Green Mountain Reservoir several sections of the river can be fished on Arapaho National Forest land. Get yourself a copy of the Arapaho National Forest map or a BLM quad for this area. Careful study will reveal places along State Highway 9 from which you may legally reach the Blue. In a few cases access may exist only to midstream. This stretch of the river is an area in which the Forest Service is acquiring land, either through trades or purchases.

Both Dillon and Green Mountain Reservoirs tend to keep water temperatures in the Blue on the cold side. Some biologists and anglers think this may inhibit the river's ability to have an abundance of insect life.

⌐ Access and Parking

The Forest Service, BLM, and CDOW each manage segments of public land along the Blue between Silverthorne and the inlet to Green Mountain Reservoir. The Blue River Campground and Boulder Creek Picnic Ground provide angling access to the river as well as camping. Check with the U.S. Forest Service Silverthorne District office for current information on access to other properties. Between Silverthorne and Green Mountain Reservoir the Colorado Division of Wildlife has several marked access points along State Highway 9 and close to the river.

Most private property along the river is well marked. Don't depend on the signs, though, because landowners are not required to post their land. Not all of the Forest Service land is well marked, either. By checking with the Forest Service, the Bureau of Land Management, and the Division of Wildlife regarding access, you will sometimes discover little-known units that are open to the public. It pays to do your research.

Blue River State Wildlife Area

Sutton Unit

The unit is 7 miles north of town. Signs mark the parking area between the road's shoulder and the Blue's left bank.

Eagles Nest Unit

The Eagles Nest unit is 9 miles north of Silverthorne and just past the Blue River Picnic Ground. The parking area, along the east side of State Highway 9, sits on a terrace above the river.

Blue River Unit

The Blue River Unit is 17 miles north from Silverthorne. This unit is west of the highway, and the road crosses the river several times. The unit gives access to the inlet of Green Mountain Reservoir.

U.S. Forest Service Land: Blue River Campground and Boulder Creek Picnic Ground

The Blue River Campground and Boulder Creek Picnic Ground provide angling access to the river as well as camping. The campground is 8 miles north of Silverthorne and is along the east side of State Highway 9. The picnic ground is a half-mile farther north.

➤ Seasons

Prior to runoff the Blue is a midge river. Flows in early spring can be low, less than 100 cfs. Downstream a few miles from town the river will still be frozen in many areas, though perhaps open in the center. Between Silverthorne and the Blue River Campground no creeks of significant size enter the Blue, so at this time the water usually runs clear in that stretch. Between ice-out and runoff anglers will have a couple of months of open-water fishing. About the time the runoff begins, the water flows increase. The river takes on some color, but as long as it's wadable, it's also fishable.

In average years the peak flows below Dillon run only a few hundred cubic feet per second. Streams entering from the high country from the east and west make the river quite dirty for a while. By midsummer the flows are on the decline, with clearing water conditions as the snowmelt ends. Water levels go back down to minimum flows in fall, and all sections of the river are easy to wade at this season.

Most sections of the river are frozen in winter. Those stretches that remain open, though, offer great cold-weather angling.

⌐ Equipment

The Blue is one of Colorado's coldest rivers, so neoprene waders will feel good in any season. The low flows of late summer, however, mean hippers are fine too. Whichever you choose, felt soles should be used.

A 4-weight rod is light enough to be sporting on this long stretch, yet heavy enough to handle the larger fish you may hook. Since most insects on the Blue run small, fine tippets—5X to 7X—will work for most fishing.

⌐ Patterns

In late spring a few mayflies join the caddis in feeding the trout. That's a time to tie on a Green Drake, Slate-Winged Mahogany, Rusty Spinner, or Red Quill.

Winter is the time for fishing midges, both adults and larvae patterns. Because of the cold the fish are lethargic and will respond primarily to a fly that is right on the nose.

Dry flies: Red Quill, Rusty Spinner, Ginger Quill, Slate-Winged Mahogany, Green Drake, caddis, midges. Nymphs: Caddis larvae, Gold-Ribbed Hare's Ear, midge larvae and emergers. Streamers: Woolly Bugger. Terrestrials: Ants, beetles.

Green Mountain Reservoir

The inlet area of the reservoir offers fly-fishing opportunities both in the lake and the river. Rising fish are a common sight

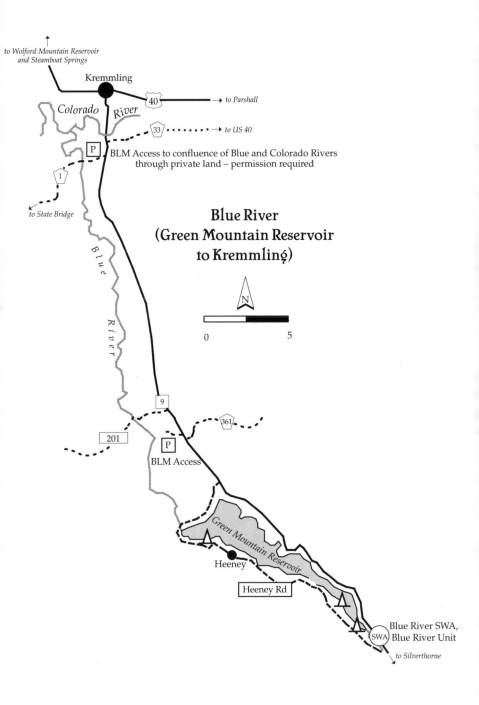

to Wolford Mountain Reservoir
and Steamboat Springs

Kremmling

Colorado *River*

40 → *to Parshall*

33 .... → *to US 40*

P BLM Access to confluence of Blue and Colorado Rivers
through private land – permission required

1

to State Bridge

Blue *River*

**Blue River
(Green Mountain Reservoir
to Kremmling)**

N

0   5

9

361

201

P
BLM Access

Green Mountain Reservoir

Heeney

Heeney Rd

SWA Blue River SWA,
Blue River Unit

to Silverthorne

during summer early and late in the day. You will have to share the water with boaters, bait and hardware fishermen, and water skiers, but browns and rainbows that grow to several pounds can make it worthwhile. As proof, nine-year-old John Clark took a 28-inch rainbow from the lake in 1990. The fish now hangs on the wall of the Clarks' family room.

One fish species fly fishermen tend to overlook is the kokanee salmon. Although they do not successfully spawn here, the fish still go through the motions each fall. Instinct compels the dark red salmon to leave the reservoir and swim upstream into the river. Because nearly all of them will die after their attempted spawn, between September 1 and January 31 the limit on them is forty fish. Kokanees are related to the sockeye salmon of the Pacific Northwest and make a very good meal. Angling methods, even during the salmon run, are restricted to artificial flies and lures. Snagging is prohibited. Contrary to common belief, kokanee will take a brightly colored fly at this time.

At Green Mountain Dam Green Mountain arises from the valley floor, appearing out of place. The river has breached the remnant of this Williams Fork Thrust Fault, and the dam is located at the south end of the mountain. The tailwater below the dam is said to have a few large fish. Access is possible but not easy due to the narrow channel and steep sides of the canyon.

A little more than 2 miles of the Blue is open to the public on Arapaho National Forest and BLM land. In the distance the river runs through a deep narrow canyon between Green Mountain and Little Green Mountain. You can reach it by foot from Green Mountain Dam or by a rough road from State Highway 9 by crossing BLM land 2 miles north of the reservoir. This stretch is said to have a few large browns. The first 2 miles past the outlet are challenging to fish because the river runs deep with a strong current that is tough to wade. There are few if any places to cross the river.

☞ Access and Parking

A 200-acre section of BLM land north of Green Mountain Reservoir connects with Arapaho National Forest land to provide access to the tailwater below the dam. A mile and a quarter past Heeney Road, which crosses the dam, and on the west side of State Highway 9 across from Forest Road 200, a poor trail leads across the sage-covered shale. The only indication that this is public land is a small BLM sign hung on the barbed-wire fence. The road ends on a terrace above the river. From here you can fish 2 miles upstream.

☞ Seasons

Because Green Mountain Reservoir serves to replace water from the Colorado Basin that is diverted to the East Slope, flows fluctuate. This situation may be improved once Muddy Creek Reservoir is on line. Check WaterTalk (see Appendix pages 152–153) for current flows before heading to this section; if it's running over 200 cfs, fishing may be impractical.

Because it's a tailwater with a strong current, the run below the dam may be open in winter. Snow and ice on the steep banks will make access challenging, so use caution.

The river here will be easiest to fish in spring and also later in the summer through the fall.

☞ Equipment

The Blue is one of Colorado's cold rivers, so neoprene waders will feel good any season. Be careful when wading this section— the channel is deep with a strong current.

A 4-weight rod is light enough to be sporting and heavy enough to handle the larger fish here.

☞ Patterns

In late spring, a few mayflies join the caddis in feeding the trout. That's a time to tie on a Green Drake, Slate-Winged Mahogany, Rusty Spinner, or a Red Quill.

Winter is the time for fishing midges, both adults and larvae patterns. Because of the cold, the fish are lethargic and respond primarily to a fly that is right on the nose.

Dry flies: Red Quill, Rusty Spinner, Ginger Quill, Slate-Winged Mahogany, Green Drake, caddis, midges. Nymphs: Caddis larvae, Gold-Ribbed Hare's Ear, midge larvae and emergers. Streamers: Woolly Bugger. Terrestrials: Ants, beetles. Salmon Flies: Brightly-colored traditional salmon patterns, Woolly Buggers, and Worm patterns in fluorescent colors.

The Confluence of the Blue and Colorado Rivers

Downstream from the public land at Green Mountain all the way to the confluence with the Colorado the Blue flows primarily through private ranchland. The predominant vegetation is sagebrush and scattered stands of cottonwoods. Terraces marking past stream levels show the extent of old meanders. A few scattered tracts of BLM land provide access to short sections of the river, but only after a long walk and careful navigation to avoid trespassing. Keep in mind that landownership changes, even of public land, with trades between landowners and federal agencies. Check the status of landownership before spending half the day getting to good-looking water only to find it is no longer accessible.

~ Access and Parking

Between Green Mountain Dam and the Colorado, the BLM controls a few scattered tracts of land on the river. Access is rather complicated, and you must first plot the tracts on a topo map and navigate with precision to avoid trespassing. A few landowners will grant permission to fish on their property. If your inquiry is

Blue River Hatch Chart												
	Jan	Feb	Mar	Apr	May	Jun	Jul	Aug	Sep	Oct	Nov	Dec
Red Quill						▓	▓	▓				
Rusty Spinner						▓	▓	▓				
Slate-Winged Mahogany						▓	▓					
Green Drake						▓	▓					
Caddis						▓	▓				▓	▓
Midges	▓	▓	▓	▓								
Ants							▓	▓	▓			

received positively, be certain to respect any restrictions the landowner requires. Your courtesy will make it possible for other anglers to enjoy access.

BLM land near the confluence with the Colorado is accessible by crossing private land with permission of the landowner. The access is located south of Kremmling and west of State Highway 9 on Grand County Road 1. Get permission at the house on the west side of the river.

➤ Seasons

Although the river is open most of the year, Murphy says it's best during spawning periods when either rainbows or browns are running upstream from the Colorado. Try to hit it when flows are running around 100 cfs.

➤ Equipment

This is a slow-moving section in many areas with deep holes, so chest waders will help you reach most of those holes.

➤ Patterns

Dry flies: Royal Wulff, Irresistible Adams, Elkhair Caddis, hoppers, Red Quill, Rusty Spinner, Ginger Quill, Slate-Winged

Mahogany, Green Drake, caddis, midges. Nymphs: Caddis larvae, Gold-Ribbed Hare's Ear, midge larvae and emergers. Streamers: Woolly Bugger. Terrestrials: Ants, beetles.

KREMMLING
TO DOTSERO

The Colorado downstream from Kremmling is large and remote. Because of its size and the lack of road access in many places, much of this section is favored for float fishing. Anglers planning to float the river between Kremmling and Glenwood Canyon should pick up a copy of a BLM publication, *The Upper Colorado River Recreation Area Kremmling to Glenwood Canyon Visitors Guide and Map.* In spite of the wordy title, it is useful to anglers who wish to enjoy this section of the river. The guide has maps of the river detailing land status, access points, and facilities, and it describes the river's rafting conditions. The book is available from BLM offices for four dollars. To order it, contact: Bureau of Land Management, 2850 Youngfield Street, Lakewood, CO 80215; (303) 239-3600.

From Gore Canyon, about 6 river miles west of State Highway 9, and all the way to Glenwood Canyon the Colorado flows through a deep but broad valley carved by the river over many eons. The land is semidesert. Scrub cedar and sagebrush is the predominant vegetation along the river.

From State Highway 9 south of Kremmling the Colorado is a navigable river open to travel with rafts, kayaks, canoes, or other suitable watercraft. Surface ownership along the river is a mix of private land, State Trust Land, State Wildlife Areas, and BLM land. Although you may legally travel on the river, you are permitted to use the shoreline only within land that is open to public access. On private land and State Trust Land not leased by CDOW you must have the landowner's or leasor's permission to fish.

Downstream from the confluence of Troublesome Creek the Colorado makes a rather abrupt change in its character. No longer is it the small, easily waded stream of Hot Sulphur Springs, or one with shallow riffles where mayflies hatch. The added flows of Troublesome Creek, the Williams Fork, the Blue River, and Muddy Creek create a major river. From where it flows beneath State Highway 9 until it reaches Glenwood Canyon the Colorado has an average width exceeding 100 feet. Regardless of its size, though, it has many runs that are wadable in late summer.

Geology influences the Colorado's nature. A few miles east of Kremmling the river leaves the igneous rock regime and enters an environment of easily eroded sedimentary rocks, sandstones, and shales. Rather than being rocky, the bottom is comprised of soft sediment. The suspended load of the river increases too, reducing water clarity.

The Colorado Division of Wildlife manages the fishery under regular bag and possession limits with no restrictions on method.

Kremmling Area

As with life-forms that become overly large, the Colorado becomes slow and lazy when it leaves Middle Park. The current seems to creep beneath the bridge on State Highway 9, being in no hurry to enter the narrow abyss of Gore Canyon.

Angling opportunities are limited in this run. The land is privately owned between Highway 9 and Gore Canyon. And although the river is navigable downstream from State Highway 9, boating isn't recommended. State Highway 9 offers the only public access to the river here. If you plan to float from near Kremmling, you will need landowner permission to exit the river because there is no public access upstream of the canyon. Gore Canyon is

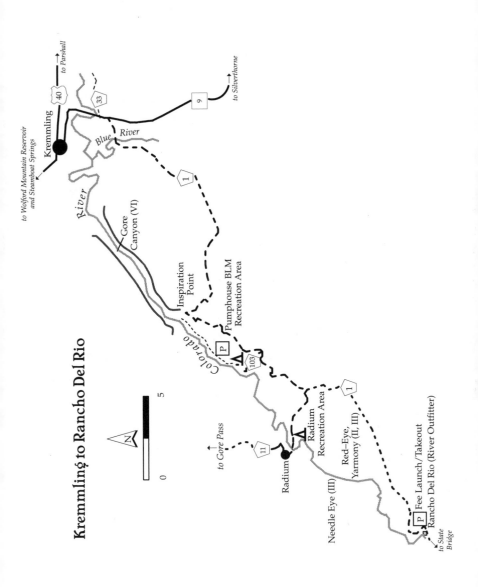

Kremmling to Rancho Del Rio

to Parshall

40

Kremmling

33

to Wolford Mountain Reservoir
and Steamboat Springs

Blue River

River

Gore Canyon (VI)

9

to Silverthorne

1

Inspiration Point

Pumphouse BLM Recreation Area

Colorado

P

103

1

N

0   5

to Gore Pass

11

Radium

Radium Recreation Area

Red-Eye, Yarmony (II, III)

Needle Eye (III)

Fee Launch/Takeout
Rancho Del Rio (River Outfitter)

P

to State Bridge

sufficiently formidable to making floating hazardous. It may make for an exciting ride for experienced white-water recreationists, but those characteristics all but eliminate fishing opportunities.

⊶ Access and Parking

A quarter-mile south of Kremmling, a BLM parking area provides fishing access on the east side of State Highway 9. On the south side of the river, the left bank, Grand County Road 33 follows the Colorado upstream to the east. At the junction of Colorado 9 and County Road 33, parking along the side of the road provides access to the left bank. These two places are the only public access points near Kremmling. Two miles east of State Highway 9 along County Road 33 there is an unmarked section of BLM land opening a few feet of the river to the public. Since the area is not marked, you must know exactly where you are to avoid trespassing.

This access is for fishing and rafting. Should you plan to float the river from here, the first public area from which to exit the river is at the BLM Pumphouse Recreation Area, 11 miles downstream. Floating this section is not recommended: The river through Gore Canyon has Class V to VI whitewater with boulderfields, waterfalls, strong currents, and steep gradients. Steep canyon walls and cliffs make portaging extremely difficult.

⊶ Seasons

This area is primarily a prerunoff and late summer through fall fishery. The river is iced over in winter, and spring runoff sees flows of 2,000 cfs in many years.

⊶ Equipment

Don't bother to wade here, because the river is too deep and the current too strong. At the BLM parking access at Kremmling the river is large with a strong current. A sinking line will be useful to get a streamer down deep. Work the water near the bank first, then cast across the current and let it drift downstream.

► Patterns

Unless a caddis hatch is coming off or you find hoppers in the hay fields, your best bet is on large streamers. Try a large Woolly Bugger or a Muddler tied with Krystal Flash. Since the water is usually a bit colored, use a pattern with some bright colors.

Pumphouse Recreation Area

Through Gore Canyon rejuvenation has returned the Colorado to a more youthful state for a few miles. Rubble eroded from uplifted granites lines the bottom. Although the river is much larger here, a 4- or 5-mile section below the canyon offers the fly fisherman a chance to drift a fly through similar but much larger structures as are in the upper river.

One thing you will notice here is that the rocks are quite slippery. I suspect that Muddy Creek has contributed to this wading dilemma. The west side of Middle Park is composed of exposures of Pierre Shale, that dark gray, almost black rock you see along the east side of State Highway 9 at Green Mountain Reservoir. The shale is composed of fine clay, which coats the river rocks, and the wading angler will find the resulting footing treacherous. This is one section of the river where cleats should help with footing. It's speculation on my part as a geologist, but I see the possibility that Wolford Mountain Reservoir may alleviate this problem; much of the fine clay Muddy Creek now dumps into the Colorado will instead settle out in the reservoir. A few high-runoff years such as the river experienced in 1984 could even flush out the existing coating of clay, making the river easier to wade.

Another thing you will notice here is that the river is large. Average flows before runoff and in late fall are around 1,000 cfs. That's a lot of water. As a result, you'll find the riffles much larger, the pools longer and deeper, and holes you will not care to fall into. The river has few places you can cross at low flow. Much of your fishing between Gore Canyon and Pumphouse will be done either from the banks or by wading out a short distance. Opportunities for dry-fly fishing are greatest in this part of the river between Gore Canyon and Radium. Midges and caddis constitute some of the more abundant insects. Because the river is so large and wading is limited in many spots to near the bank, a heavy rod will be invaluable. An 8- or 9-weight will make it much easier to get your fly to the runs you can't reach by wading.

Structures come on a large scale here, too. In the upper river large boulders divide the current. Below the canyon, islands serve the same purpose. The points of the islands, both the upstream and downstream ends, are places you want to concentrate on. The deep holes are places through which you'll want to drift a large streamer or leech pattern.

Downstream from Pumphouse the river is too large to wade in most runs. A raft will become your best means of access. (You will find little access from the road between Radium and State Bridge.) Because few serious hazards exist on this sixty-plus miles of water, competent rafters can enjoy extended float trips on the river. The majority of the land is public and controlled by the BLM. Primitive campsites along the river allow for overnight stays. Takeout points let you plan trips varying from one day to a week.

Between Pumphouse and Radium, 4 miles downstream, the river is rated Class II, and the Needle Eye Rapid is Class III. There is a warm spring on the left bank below the rapid at the foot of the cliffs. There's also poison ivy here. Two river campsites, Cabin and Cottonwood, are located between miles 14 and 15, 1 mile upstream from the Radium Recreation Area.

Between Radium and State Bridge most of the land along the river is managed by the BLM. Between miles 17 and 18 on the river you will encounter Yarmony Rapid in Red Gorge. It's listed as a Class II/III rapid with hazardous flows. Three camping and picnic sites are located along the river in this section.

➤ Access and Parking

The Pumphouse Recreation Area access road is located 13 miles west of State Highway 9 along Grand County Road 1 (also identified as Trough Road on some maps). Pumphouse has parking, two developed launch areas, and twelve developed campsites with picnic tables and fireplaces, toilets, and drinking water. During the summer a BLM river ranger lives on the site. From Pumphouse, the Gore Canyon Hiking Trail follows the left bank upstream on the south side of the river a couple miles to fishing and primitive camping sites.

When the river is running too high to cross, the right bank (north side) can be reached through the Radium State Wildlife Area. From Trough Road, take County Road 11 to Radium, then head north. About 3 miles north of Radium take the right fork, which heads east toward the river. When this road is wet, a four-wheel-drive vehicle is essential.

➤ Seasons

The section between Gore Canyon and Pumphouse will be running between 400 and 700 cfs prior to the spring runoff. Mild overcast days can bring out midge hatches. Very high flows and brown water predominate beginning in May. Peak flows recorded at Pumphouse have exceeded 12,000 cfs. Go somewhere else once the runoff begins.

Because the Colorado drains such a large area, flows remain high through summer, but float fishing is again possible by July in most years. The river is subject to rapid rises and dirty water conditions through summer from thunderstorms. By late summer, flows usually decline to less than 1,100 cfs.

Some anglers believe fall is the best time to fish this river. It is a good time to try for spawning browns, especially near tributary streams such as the Piney River at State Bridge. The crowds begin to taper off, and anglers will find many places to fish with no competition. Flows are down to a minimum by late fall, about 400 cfs.

Unlike much of the river, which is closed by ice through the winter, the stretch between Pumphouse and Radium is usually open, though ice forms along the banks for several feet into the stream. Winter fishing here can be good with nymphs.

⇥ Equipment

Except during low flows, the river has few places from which to cross it. Chest waders are advised, though, because the water is deep and the current strong. Because the bottom is slippery, cleats or a wading staff are essential. Because of the river's width (in excess of 100 feet) and windy conditions in the canyon in spring and winter, a 9-foot rod, 6- to 9-weight, is a reasonable choice. This makes it much easier to reach the runs that are too deep to wade. For late summer and fall dry-fly fishing, a 4-weight should be fine, provided you can get close enough to the fish. Since the water is usually a bit murky even at its clearest, you can get away with using a 4X or 5X tippet except when fishing #22 midge patterns.

⇥ Patterns

Caddis imitations are good, as are midge patterns most of the year. Evergreen fly fisherman Larry Flowers recommends using a Prince Nymph for subsurface action or an Elkhair Caddis on top when the fish are feeding on adults. Try a large Woolly Bugger or a Muddler tied with Krystal Flash. Since the water is usually a bit colored, use a pattern with some bright colors.

Radium to State Bridge

Between Radium and Rancho Del Rio runs 6 miles of river that is inaccessible by road. All but the last half-mile of the river borders public land at least along one side. This is the longest stretch of the Colorado with no road access. Because most of the land is controlled by the BLM, lunch stops and camping along the banks are permitted.

Rancho Del Rio is located at mile 21.5, where you can take out or put in. Services here include gas, limited groceries, equipment and vehicle storage, toilets and dressing rooms, parking, and shuttle service for a fee.

Downstream from Rancho Del Rio the Colorado runs along Eagle County Road 11, and there are many places to park within a short walk of the water. Even though the river here is large, there are quite a few places to wade, at least in the spring when the ice is gone and after the runoff. Wading fishermen should search out the faster currents near shallow areas and drift nymphs through them. Keep in mind that this is large water and work it thoroughly.

A mile of the Colorado upstream from State Bridge may be reached on foot by an abandoned section of the former county road. Driving the old road is not recommended.

The Piney River joins the Colorado from the south at State Bridge. This is an area that Eddie Kochman, fisheries manager at CDOW, says has some big browns. At low flows in late summer the river can be waded, though it may not be possible to cross it here. Although it's large, you should fish it the same as you would similar water in Middle Park. The water easiest to wade is on the south side. Work your fly through the faster current at the edges of the slow shallow water.

State Bridge is named for the bridge built in 1892 across the Colorado. The greatly deteriorated remains of the structure still

The Colorado River upstream from State Bridge can be waded in late summer.

stand a short distance upstream from the highway. It was rebuilt in 1915 and again in 1917 following major floods. In 1966 the current structure replaced it.

➤ Access and Parking

Radium is located at mile 15.5 downstream from State Highway 9. By road it's about 16 miles from State Highway 9 over Grand County Road 1 to County Road 11. From there, it's 2 miles to the Radium Recreation Area. Facilities include a boat launch/takeout, toilets, parking, and camping.

Rancho Del Rio is 6 miles by river and 5 miles along Eagle County Road 11 (Trough Road) from the junction of Grand County Roads 1 and 11.

The State Bridge launch/takeout site is located at State Highway 131 and Trough Road at mile 25.2 by river from State Highway 9. State Bridge is 15 miles north of Interstate 70 from the

Wolcott exit. Other facilities here include parking, toilets, showers, and cabins for a fee.

➤ Seasons

Fishing time downstream from Radium is limited because the river is usually iced over in winter. Open water arrives as early as March, giving the angler a good six to eight weeks of early-season fishing in the spring. Runoff keeps the river high into midsummer. It also comes up fast and gets dirty following thunderstorms. Once the runoff ends the Colorado begins to clear as the flows continue to decline. From summer through fall the river offers some of the finest fishing of the year.

➤ Equipment

Due to the long stretches of water with little or no access from the roads, a raft is the most useful piece of equipment here. Don't forget the oars. You will pass many camping sites along the way, so bring camping gear too.

When floating this stretch in a raft or driftboat, consider rigging up two rods. Set up a heavier rod—6- through 9-weight—to fish deep with streamers or nymphs in the fast sections. The other rod—a 4- or 5-weight—should be rigged for dry-fly fishing. Depending on the season, tie on a midge or Elkhair Caddis or other caddis imitation for fishing the long slow runs. Cast the caddis over close to the bank. Evening in late summer and fall is good for fishing to trout feeding on bugs along the brush-lined river edge. Water temperatures in late summer and early fall are warm enough to wade wet if you're so inclined.

➤ Patterns

The best dry flies are small midges and Elkhair Caddises in large sizes—12–16—in spring and fall. For fishing deep, use large streamers such as Woolly Buggers and Muddler Minnows, and large Prince Nymphs.

State Bridge to Dotsero

Downstream from State Bridge, fishing access is primarily by raft or driftboat. In general, you will find three types of water between here and Dotsero: long, slow, deep flat runs; broad meanders, and mild-to-challenging rapids. The appearance of the current can fool you—it is much stronger than it looks. Though you can fish the entire river in this section, there is a good amount of private land surrounding it. Unless you have permission, do not venture onto the private land.

The Colorado adds the flows of several small streams in this stretch, making it an even larger river. In a few places the road deviates from the river and access is blocked by private property. But for most of the length between State Bridge and Dotsero Eagle County Road 301 parallels the river. You will find plenty of parking places, both wide areas along the road and on crude two-track paths leading toward the water. You will need to cross the railroad tracks to reach the river in this stretch, so be careful.

Derby Creek joins the Colorado River at Burns. Although it's a small stream, the headwaters offer some great lake fishing for rainbows and cutthroats. County and Forest Service roads (four-wheel-drive) end at the Flat Tops Wilderness Area boundary. Trails from Crescent and Mackinaw Lakes lead up onto the plateau to Island Lakes and Deer Lake. Emerald Lake, beside Forest Road 613, has good fishing for small brookies.

⌁ Access and Parking

The State Bridge launch/takeout site is located at State Highway 131 and Trough Road at mile 25.2 by river from State Highway 9. State Bridge is 15 miles north of Interstate 70 from the Wolcott exit. Other facilities here include parking, toilets, showers, and cabins for a fee.

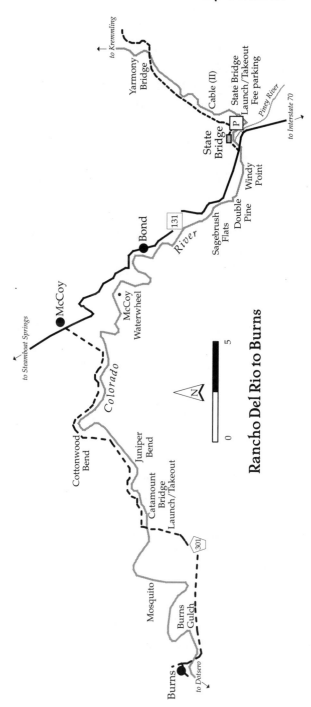

to Kremmling

Yarmony Bridge

Cable (II)

State Bridge Launch/Takeout
Fee parking

Piney River

to Interstate 70

State Bridge

P

Windy Point

Double Pine

Sagebrush Flats

131

Bond

River

McCoy

McCoy Waterwheel

to Steamboat Springs

Colorado

Cottonwood Bend

Juniper Bend

Catamount Bridge Launch/Takeout

301

N

0   5

Rancho Del Rio to Burns

Mosquito

Burns Gulch

Burns

to Dotsero

Between State Bridge and Bond, at mile 28 beside State Highway 131, rafters pass the Windy Point Site at mile 25.8. It features a natural boat landing and primitive campsites. The site is also reached by a crude four-wheel-drive road along the left bank of the river from State Bridge. The next places to stop are Double Pine at mile 26.7 and Sagebrush Flat at mile 27.4. These have no facilities other than primitive campsites.

At Bond, an old railroad town, services are limited to gas, telephone, a post office, and groceries. Downstream to Catamount the most severe water is rated Class II. You'll see the largest waterwheel in Colorado at mile 31.7 near McCoy. Eale Brooks built it in 1922 to lift water to irrigate his homestead, located on a terrace above the river. The waterwheel has been restored and is listed in the National Register of Historic Places.

Riverside facilities are limited to primitive camp and picnic sites at The Landing Strip, mile 33.8; Cottonwood Bend, mile 36; and Juniper Bend, mile 38. The Catamount Bridge Site is located at mile 39.6, or 7 miles west of State Highway 131 on Eagle County Road 301. The launch site has toilets, parking, and undeveloped campsites. The river in this area is rated Class I/II. The Mosquito Site, mile 41.2, and Burns Gulch Site, mile 44, offer primitive camping and picnic stops along the river.

At mile 44.5, 0.2-mile west of Burns Store, is a small campsite and public river access. Burns Store has groceries, gas, a pay telephone, and rental cabins. There's also a post office on the east end of the community.

The river down to Derby Creek is Class II with a Class III drop over large boulders at Rodeo Rapid, mile 45.2. The BLM suggests you scout the rapid before running it.

At Derby Junction along Eagle County Road 301, go west on County Road 39 for 6 miles to Forest Road 613. When it's wet, you will need good-traction tires or possibly chains, because it turns to grease. This four-wheel-drive road ends at Crescent and Mackinaw

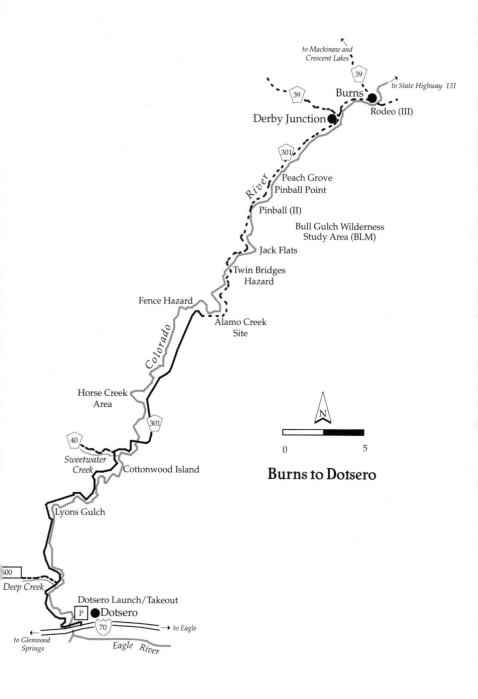

to Mackinaw and
Crescent Lakes

39

39

to State Highway 131

Burns

Derby Junction ●

Rodeo (III)

301

River

Peach Grove
Pinball Point

Pinball (II)

Bull Gulch Wilderness
Study Area (BLM)

Jack Flats

Twin Bridges
Hazard

Fence Hazard

Colorado

Alamo Creek
Site

Horse Creek
Area

301

40

N

Sweetwater
Creek

Cottonwood Island

0   5

Lyons Gulch

Burns to Dotsero

500

Deep Creek

Dotsero Launch/Takeout

P ● Dotsero

70

to Eagle

to Glenwood
Springs

Eagle River

Lakes about 11 miles from County Road 39. Trail 1857 climbs the canyon wall to Island Lakes. Follow Trail 1802 north 2 miles to Deer Lake.

The next camp and picnic site is at Peach Grove, mile 48. There are no facilities. Pinball Point is the first site downstream from Burns with a launch/takeout area. It also has parking and temporary toilets. The river is still Class II here, but there are hazards below Pinball Point Rapid at mile 49.4 and Twin Bridges at mile 52. The land south of the river between Pinball Rapid and Jack Flats, mile 51, is a Wilderness Study Area (WSA). You can camp and picnic here and enjoy the hiking trails in the Bull Gulch WSA, but the site has no facilities.

The Alamo Creek Site, mile 53.7, has a boat ramp, parking, and temporary toilets, all by arrangement with the landowner. The right-of-way is temporary and subject to change. The water is Class II. Watch for a bridge hazard at mile 53.9 and a fence at mile 54.6, at which you are advised to keep to the left.

Along the Horse Creek area, at miles 56.2, 56.6, 58, and 58.3 you'll find primitive camping, picnic areas, and hiking trails. Most of the land between miles 52 and 63 is private, with some short stretches of BLM access on the riverbanks.

Sweetwater Creek enters the Colorado at mile 60.8. There is no launch access here because the land is private. Adjacent land upstream does have limited parking along Eagle County Road 301 for fishing access.

Cottonwood Island Site, mile 61.8, has a launch/takeout area, parking, and primitive camping. The river in this section is Class II.

The site at mile 64 has a launch/takeout, parking, bulletin board, toilets, and primitive camping and picnic sites. A four-wheel-drive trail to the west leads to hiking and bike paths in juniper-covered hills.

Downstream at mile 66.2 Coffeepot Road follows Deep Creek, providing access to the southeast side of the Flat Tops Wilderness Area.

The Dotsero launch site is located at the river along U.S. 6, just north of Interstate 70. Parking and temporary toilets are located here. A quarter-mile downstream the Eagle River joins the Colorado.

➤ Seasons

Fishing on this stretch is limited to the prerunoff period in spring and midsummer through fall. Because the river is uncontrolled, even in summer heavy thunderstorms can cause the Colorado to rise quickly and remain discolored by a heavy load of sediment for several days. Fall brings some of the most pleasant days on the river. After Labor Day summer's heat abates, and flows no longer present serious hazards to rafters. The water is as clear as it ever gets in fall, though it always appears colored with sediment to a degree. Afternoon caddis hatches offer good dry-fly fishing. Late in the year winter closes most of the river.

Here are the average flows you can expect at Dotsero throughout the year. January to February: 800–900 cfs; March to April: 900–1,800 cfs; May to June: 4,000–6,000 cfs; July to September: 3,000–1,200 cfs; October to December: 1,000–1,300 cfs.

ROCK CREEK

(See map for Wolford Mountain Reservoir and Rock Creek, page 69.)

Rock Creek's headwaters begin a few miles north of State Highway 134. After collecting the flows of a good number of small streams it becomes a creek with significant volume and thus turns into an attractive small stream. About 20 feet wide in most places, Rock Creek has quite a variety of water for such a small stream.

A mile south of 134 it meanders through a broad meadow. After another mile it enters a rejuvenated canyon, one that's steep-sided and deep. Here the only access is by foot. The canyon extends several miles through wilderness before emerging near the town of McCoy on State Highway 131, north of State Bridge. From McCoy, Rock Creek runs through a beautiful pasture to reach the Colorado.

Rock Creek has naturally reproducing populations of brook, brown, and cutthroat trout. Rainbows have been stocked in summers past, and some hold over or do well. Most fish are small, but a few browns exceed 12 inches.

The upper reaches of Rock Creek's source tumble through long curving ridges, steep-sided timbered valleys, and occasional open meadows. The lower runs move through a deep narrow canyon. This is where you'll find the best fishing if you're up to the challenge.

Most of the stream is small with lots of meanders and holes left from washed-out beaver ponds. Beavers are active on the stream and have built low impoundments; however, few are more than 3 feet deep. The canyon section contains a series of riffles

An angler hooks a brown in Rock Creek.

and plunges, along with a few small deep pools. Access is generally difficult because of the steep walls that are covered with nearly impenetrable brush. In many places the only access is through the stream.

The headwaters and upper reaches of Rock Creek are on U.S. Forest Service land within the Routt National Forest. Upstream from McCoy to the forest boundary the land is a mix of BLM, State Trust, and private lands with very little public access. The Gore Pass area has a good population of deer and elk and attracts a large number of hunters beginning with the archery season in August. Hunting seasons run through November. Because of the many small out-of-the-way streams in the region, it's a good place to spend a weekend or longer. In addition to U.S. Forest Service campgrounds, there are plenty of places for more remote camping.

⌐ Access and Parking

From Kremmling, go west on U.S. 40 6 miles to the junction of State Highway 134. After crossing Gore Pass, continue west 7 miles past the summit to Forest Road 206. Follow it a mile south to the meadow section, or continue south another half-mile to a parking area beside Shoe and Stocking Creek. Other parking sites are scattered along the creek.

⌐ Seasons

Runoff begins early in this drainage. Rock Creek runs high and dirty as soon as it's accessible in the spring. By mid-June the creek starts to clear and fishing gets good. It's usually at its best after July 4. By August the best fishing is down in the canyon, several miles below the parking area at Shoe and Stocking Creek. Fall fishing for spawning browns can be good. Forget it after October.

⌐ Equipment

If you own a lightweight rod, even as small as a 1- or 2-weight, you are in for some fun on Rock Creek. Such rods should handle the 9- to 16-inch browns that will take a well-presented fly.

The creek is small and easily managed in hip waders.

⌐ Patterns

Your choice should lean toward the smaller patterns, but even a #14 Humpy works well. Because the best angling occurs in mid-summer immediately following runoff, dry flies produce best results. Rock Creek isn't hatch-matching water. In addition to Humpys, stock your fly box with Adamses, Elkhair Caddises, Royal Wulffs, and terrestrial patterns such as ants and grasshoppers.

EAGLE RIVER

The Eagle River gets its start along U.S. 24 on the west slope of Tennessee Pass. Between its head and the confluence with Gore Creek west of Vail, the geology of the region prevents it from being more than a put-and-take fishery. Along Interstate 70 west of U.S. 24, though, the Eagle is a classic Western fly-fishing river.

This river can be challenging to wade. Algae clings to the rocks, making them very slippery. Felt soles may not be adequate to keep you from sliding around, and you might want to use cleats for a surefooted grip, along with a wading staff. East of Gypsum the Eagle has a high gradient, adding to difficulties wading anglers will experience.

Through the winter most of the Eagle freezes. A few spring holes keep the river open in spots. By March the river begins to open and offers angling until the runoff starts. Milk Creek, west of Wolcott, was once a major source of calcium sulfate, a mineral that gives water the appearance of chocolate milk following thunderstorms. A few years back the Colorado Division of Wildlife constructed small structures on Milk Creek to settle out the sediment. They also keep the Eagle relatively clear after a rain. It can still get dirty from other sources, but the situation is not as bad as before.

Quite a few smaller streams run into the Eagle, the best probably being Gore Creek. It's a Gold Medal stream through Vail, between Red Sandstone Creek and its confluence with the Eagle. Gore Creek holds all four primary species of trout: brook, brown, cutthroat, and rainbow. They feed on an assortment of caddis,

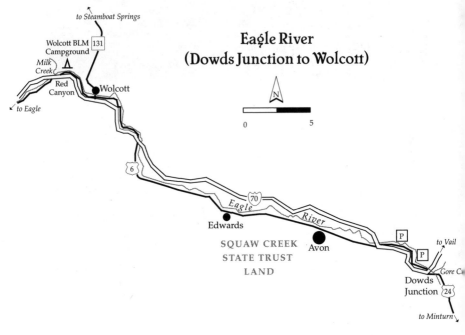

mayflies, and stoneflies. Fishing in Gore Creek is restricted to flies and lures with a limit of two trout of 16 inches or larger.

The mountains east and south of the Eagle's valley were glaciated during the ice ages of a few thousand years ago. As the glaciers melted, the outwash scoured out the river's present channel while depositing large rocks in the valley. The river has cut down through the valley, leaving low terraces. West of Avon, the valley opens up, and the Eagle meanders more broadly through pastures and hay meadows.

West of Dowds Junction on Interstate 70, the first 2 miles of river cross the White River National Forest. From there to its confluence with the Colorado, the Eagle flows through a mix of private property with some BLM land. Colorado Division of Wildlife and State Trust Land properties, however, give the angler access to several miles of the river.

The Eagle has no special angling restrictions other than a two-fish limit.

Public water on the Eagle River near Wolcott.

➤ Access and Parking

From the junction of Interstate 70 and U.S. 24 west of the town of Vail, the interstate and U.S. 6 follow the course of the Eagle. You can see the river from the interstate but will need to get onto U.S. 6 to reach the river. U.S. 24 runs parallel to the Eagle from its head near Tennessee Pass to the Interstate 70–U.S. 6 junction.

Squaw Creek State Trust Land, Exit 163 from I-70 From Edwards, go south to the signal light, then west on U.S. 6 for 2 miles to the bridge crossing the river. This provides access to about 1.25 miles of the Eagle.

Wolcott Campground, U.S. 6 This BLM campground off U.S. 6 near Wolcott provides access to 0.5-mile of the river.

Red Canyon, U.S. 6 One and a half miles of water are open to anglers along the old highway on BLM land. It's about 3 miles west of Wolcott.

Eagle River State Wildlife Area, U.S. 6 The river is open from about 0.5-mile west of the town of Eagle and 5 miles

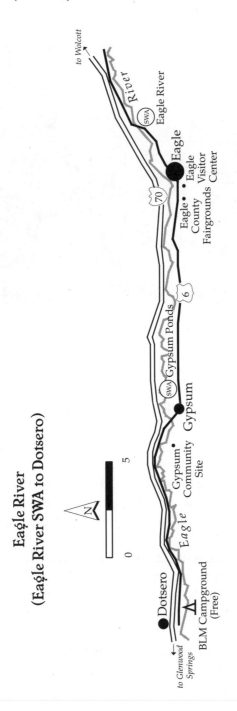

Eagle River
(Eagle River SWA to Dotsero)

upstream along U.S. 6. Several parking pullouts are found along the highway.

Eagle Visitors Center, Exit 147 Take the south frontage road west from exit 147. Public access opens about 0.2-mile of the river along the north bank.

Eagle County Fairgrounds, Exit 147 The river is 0.3-mile west of the visitor center on the frontage road. Parking is located on the river's north bank. County property opens about 1.5 miles to the west and to the center of the river.

Gypsum Ponds State Wildlife Area, Exit 140 From exit 140, go east about 0.3-mile on the paved road south of Interstate 70 to the CDOW property. The wildlife area opens 2.5 miles on the north side of the Eagle.

Gypsum Community Site, Exit 140 Go 1 mile west of Gypsum on the south frontage road. BLM land provides access to about 2 miles of the river.

➤ Seasons

Before the spring runoff, the Eagle fishes well on nymphs. Flows start increasing from their winter low of less than 200 cfs to about 400 cfs. By May, runoff takes it up to 1,300 cfs, so it's best to go somewhere else then.

The runoff peaks in June with flows close to 3,000 cfs. Caddis hatches get started in June too. Pale morning duns follow in July. Because the river is uncontrolled, the flows are still high though declining by midsummer. After July 4 the river should be clearing. But it can still exceed 1,000 cfs, so be careful when wading.

By August and September the river can be pleasant. The flows are down and the water is clear. *Baetis* come along in early fall. It's a great time to hit the river because summer tourists are gone, kids are in school, and best of all, the fall colors are at a peak. The fish are hungry too, and cooperative. Fishing will continue to be good into October.

ᴇ Equipment

The two most important items for much of this river are felt soles for your wading shoes and a wading staff. You may also want cleats or studs on the felt soles.

ᴇ Patterns

Dry flies: Blue-Winged Olive, Elkhair Caddis, Humpy, Yellow Sally, Sofa Pillow, Griffith Gnat. Nymphs: Halfback, Twenty-Incher, Prince, Bitch Creek, Golden Stone, Little Yellow Stone, caddis larvae, midge larvae.

Eagle River Hatch Chart												
	Jan	Feb	Mar	Apr	May	Jun	Jul	Aug	Sep	Oct	Nov	Dec
Blue-Winged Olive		■	■	■					■	■	■	
Red Quill							■	■				
Green Drake							■	■				
Caddis						■	■	■	■	■		
Midges			■	■	■	■	■	■	■	■	■	

THE LOWER RIVER— GLENWOOD CANYON TO RIFLE

A study of the average flows of the Colorado at Glenwood Springs suggests that fly-fishing opportunities are more limited here than on other sections of the river. As though to make up for the rather limited periods when the river is relatively low and clear, it holds large trout, perhaps some of the largest on average in the Colorado.

The river usually remains open throughout the year west of Glenwood Springs. Ice may form along the banks during the coldest months, but it's rare for this stretch to freeze solid. In Glenwood Canyon cold temperatures and short periods of sunlight allow the river to freeze over in winter.

Glenwood Canyon

Downstream from the confluence with the Eagle, the Colorado enters Glenwood Canyon, an area of outstanding beauty. The deep narrow gorge was created by the uplift of the Flat Tops Plateau.

Shoshone Dam in Glenwood Canyon forms a small impoundment. It's not a reservoir—the river does move here, though slowly. Below the diversion the stream is dewatered most of the year, the runoff period excepted. After operating the Public Service Company's generators, the water is returned to the stream. Rapids and cascades make it impractical to fish very far above the Grizzly Creek confluence.

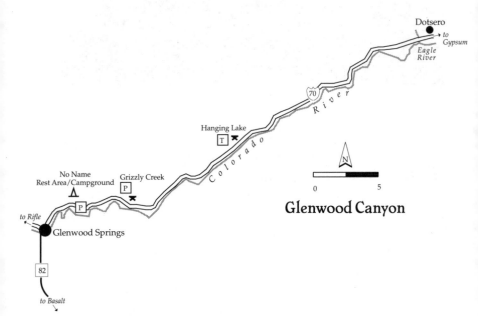

Glenwood Canyon

In Glenwood Canyon land ownership is a mix of public and private. The Bureau of Land Management has land at the east and west ends of the canyon and between Glenwood Springs and Chacra, 8 miles to the west. Through the canyon, the Forest Service controls the land except for three small privately owned tracts. West of Rifle the Colorado Division of Wildlife controls a mile of the river at the Hunt State Wildlife Area.

Through Glenwood Canyon fishing is limited by the difficult access. West of Glenwood Springs the size of the river places its own restrictions on fishing. There are few places that can be easily waded.

Even though the flows start picking up in April, you'll want to fish the caddis hatch then. Driving through the area at night will remind you of driving through a blizzard.

➣ Access and Parking

Interstate 70 follows the course of the Colorado from Dotsero to the Utah Line. Through Glenwood Canyon the new highway limits river access to a few parking areas. A bike path, though, does run through the canyon along the river. Access to the path is available at Blair Ranch (exit 129), Hanging Lake trailhead (exit 125), Grizzly Creek Rest Area (exit 121), and No Name Rest Area (exit 119).

At the west end of the canyon and at Glenwood Springs you can put in rafts to fish or just to enjoy a float. The river is slow with gentle meanders and riffles, and there is little white water after runoff. Floating the river offers the only access to the entire stretch between the canyon and Rifle.

➣ Seasons

Fishing in the canyon is limited to spring before the runoff, to summer following runoff, and to fall. Browns become active in late summer, and dry-fly action can be good at that time. Ice in the winter and high, dangerous flows in May and June (and at times in July) inhibit angling opportunities.

➣ Equipment

There is very little water suitable for wading in the canyon with the exception of the area around No Name Rest Area. Even there, don't consider wading until well after the runoff is over and flows are manageable.

➣ Patterns

Dry flies: Yellow Sally, Sofa Pillow, Elkhair Caddis, Humpy, Griffith Gnat, grasshopper imitations. Nymphs: Halfback, Twenty-Incher, Prince, Bitch Creek, Golden Stone, Little Yellow Stone, caddis larvae, midge larvae. Streamers: Muddler Minnow, Woolly Bugger.

Glenwood Springs to Rifle

West of Glenwood Springs the Colorado River valley opens into a broad sloping canyon. By the time the river passes Rifle, it flows through an expansive plain. West of the canyon, the Colorado once again becomes a free-running stream, its bottom lined with cobbles and boulders. The habitat is suitable for stoneflies, which are abundant. For most of the year anglers will do best using large nymphs and streamers. With the exception of the caddis, stonefly, and midge hatches, dry-fly angling is not as productive.

The river here is large, and floating is likely the best way to fish it. Except during runoff the rapids aren't severe. The current is strong, though, making wade-fishing hazardous except along the banks in a few places. The fish in this part of the Colorado tend to move around a lot and concentrate as groups in whatever hole suits their mood for the day. You'll have to fish a lot of water to find them, but when you do, you'll find several together.

Downstream from the confluence with the Eagle River the Colorado is managed to allow a regular limit of trout, and there are no restrictions on method.

⮞ Access and Parking

Interstate 70 follows the course of the Colorado west of Glenwood Springs. U.S. 6 and county roads provide access and parking near the river.

At the west end of the canyon and at Glenwood Springs you can put in rafts for fishing or just floating. The river is slow with gentle meanders and riffles, and there is little white water after runoff. Floating the river offers the only access to the entire stretch between the canyon and Rifle. Be extremely careful on the river during runoff or any other high-water period because the currents then can be dangerous.

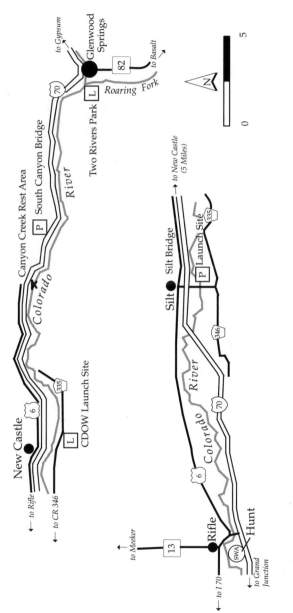

Glenwood Springs to Rifle

West of Glenwood Springs the river's current is too strong for wading. This is prime floating water.

Glenwood Springs, Exit 116 from I-70 Anglers have access to both the Roaring Fork and the Colorado at Two Rivers Park in town. Rafters can put in here.

South Canyon Bridge, Exit 111 from I-70 The bridge across the Colorado leads to a road to the south following South Canyon Creek. Anglers have foot access along the north (right) bank of the river from a BLM parking area.

Canyon Creek Rest Area The rest area is located beside the eastbound lanes of Interstate 70 about 1.5 miles west of exit 111.

New Castle, Exit 105 The Colorado Division of Wildlife has a boat launch and picnic area along the south (left) bank of the Colorado. Get off Interstate 70 at the New Castle exit, go south to Garfield County Road 345, then west to the parking area at the Garfield Creek State Wildlife Area.

Silt Bridge, Exit 97 From the exit, cross the first bridge. A parking area and boat launch site are on the west side of the road.

Hunt State Wildlife Area, Exit 90 At the Rifle exit, take the service road along the river that leads to a visitor center and rest stop.

⮞ Seasons

Downstream from Glenwood Springs the Colorado is open almost year-round. Late summer and fall may be the best times to fish it.

In the Glenwood Springs area a caddis hatch usually comes off in April. Even so, the river can be challenging. Try to fish it with someone who knows its idiosyncrasies. Once the runoff begins the river isn't fishable until July or August at best—there's just too much water. Flows vary from 1,300 cfs in winter to around 10,000 cfs during runoff.

⮞ Equipment

A rod capable of making long casts will be an advantage in this section. Large stonefly nymphs and streamers will be used most often, so 6-weight and heavier rods are ideal.

In general, the river is too large to wade except close to the banks, provided it's shallow. Since the river is navigable, anglers fishing from a raft will be able to cover much more water than will those fishing from the banks.

⮞ Patterns

Dry flies: Yellow Sally, Sofa Pillow, Elkhair Caddis, Humpy, Griffith Gnat, grasshopper imitations. Nymphs: Halfback, Twenty-Incher, Prince, Bitch Creek, Golden Stone, Little Yellow Stone, caddis larvae, midge larvae. Streamers: Muddler Minnow, Woolly Bugger.

THE ROARING FORK
OF THE COLORADO RIVER

The Ute Indians were among the earliest recorded people to inhabit the area around Glenwood Springs. They named the Roaring Fork "Thunder River" with good reason. The Roaring Fork is a boisterous river. Even from a distance its current is audible.

From the headwaters near Independence Pass to the confluence with the Colorado the Roaring Fork is a free-flowing river, making it unique. Few rivers in the state are completely free of dams, though the Fork does have many irrigation diversions. It's one of the few floatable rivers in the state. From its beginnings to the Colorado River the Fork is only about 70 miles long. It has big fish, too.

If you're not accustomed to fishing large streams, the Fork can intimidate you. Its current is strong. The water is often slightly off-color, hiding deep holes. Footing can be tricky on its rocky bottom. One thing in its favor is that the river fishes well nearly all year.

Rainbows and browns are the predominant species in the Roaring Fork. The upper stretches have small brookies: According to the Colorado Division of Wildlife, they average 12 to 18 inches. From my experience this is no bureaucratic exaggeration. In the river upstream of Glenwood Springs to around Carbondale you'll find many whitefish and suckers. They also readily take a fly and fight well.

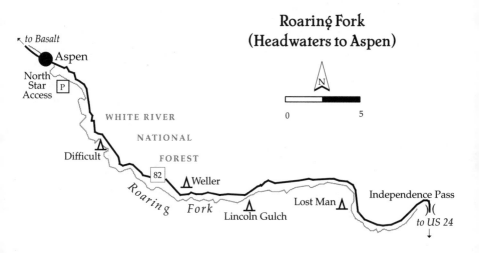

Roaring Fork
(Headwaters to Aspen)

The Headwaters

From its headwaters a mile north of Independence Pass downstream to Aspen, the Roaring Fork runs through the White River National Forest. Not until it is within 3 miles of Aspen does the stream cross private land, with the exception of a few private holdings within the forest. The headwaters section upstream from Aspen is managed to allow a regular limit of trout with no restrictions on method. The river is small and holds lots of pan-sized brookies, along with rainbows.

➤ Access and Parking

State Highway 82 east of Aspen follows the river to its headwaters near Independence Pass.

White River National Forest Forest Service campgrounds provide access and parking in addition to the road shoulders.

West of the summit of the pass several patented mining claims are the most common private holdings along the river within the national forest. Although these may not always be posted against trespass, it is still illegal to do so. In many cases mines are no longer active, and in some areas old shafts (vertical holes) may have caved in but could appear solid on the surface. They can be unstable, presenting the possibility of an unseen hazard. Use caution if you decide to fish these stretches of the Fork.

North Star Access There is county property along both sides of the river here, 2 miles east of Aspen along State Highway 82. The half-mile stretch is well marked.

❧ Seasons

Because of the high elevation, this stretch offers summer angling after runoff extending into fall.

❧ Equipment

Because this section is primarily a small-stream brookie fishery, it's a place to use light tackle. Hip waders should be adequate.

❧ Patterns

Little brookies are seldom picky. Dry flies and nymphs should be small, #14–#20.

Aspen to Basalt

Downstream from Aspen the Fork becomes a meandering meadow stream. The gradient is less than in the headwaters though still significant: The river drops about 1,000 feet in 15 miles. You will find lots of riffle sections with a few pools. This

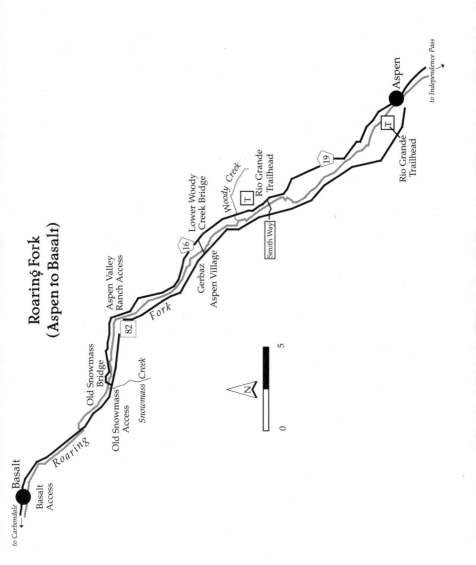

Roaring Fork
(Aspen to Basalt)

to Carbondale

Basalt

Basalt Access

Roaring

Old Snowmass Bridge

Old Snowmass Access

Snowmass Creek

82

Fork

Aspen Valley Ranch Access

Gerbaz

Aspen Village

16

Lower Woody Creek Bridge

Woody Creek

Smith Way

T

Rio Grande Trailhead

19

Rio Grande Trailhead

T

Aspen

to Independence Pass

N

0   5

stretch of the river is fishable for most of the year. Even though it runs through private property, several areas are open to the public.

Between Hallam Lake in Aspen and Upper Woody Creek Bridge the river is designated as Wild Trout Water. From McFarlane Creek to Upper Woody Creek Bridge angling is permitted with flies and lures only. All fish caught in this section must be released unharmed. Below the bridge and downstream to the confluence with the Colorado River, fishing methods are still restricted to flies and lures, but two fish over 16 inches may be kept.

➤ Access and Parking

State Highway 82 follows the south side of the river between Basalt and Aspen. Pitkin County Road 19 runs north and parallel to the river but a short distance away. Both roads provide access to open sections of the Fork.

Aspen Area The Rio Grande Trail Access is between Hallam (some sources spell it "Holum") Lake near Aspen, downstream to Upper Woody Creek Bridge. Access is along the north side of the Roaring Fork and extends from Upper Woody Creek Bridge downstream to 500 feet. This makes 5.5 miles of river accessible on the right (north) bank.

Lower Woody Creek Bridge Access (Gerbaz and Aspen Village) Between Gerbaz and Aspen Village, go north off State Highway 82 to the Roaring Fork and Lower Woody Creek Bridge. Fishing access is upstream for 2 miles along the south bank. Starting 100 feet downstream from the bridge, anglers can fish the north bank for 0.75-mile.

Other Access Some sources mention additional access points in this area. One is the Aspen River Valley Ranch between mile markers 28 and 29 on State Highway 82. Another is Old Snowmass, at the junction of State Highway 82 and Pitkin County Road 11, downstream from the Old Snowmass Bridge. A mile of the river is open between Old Snowmass Bridge and Lazy Glen Trailer Park.

➤ Seasons

This stretch is open for most of the year. It offers good fishing even during the spring runoff if the river is reasonably clear. In the summer you will find good fly fishing here when other sections of the river become too warm. Although it is not known as a winter fishery, open runs can be worth trying then.

➤ Equipment

The Fork's slippery rounded rocks make for interesting wading unless you have felt soles or studs.

➤ Patterns

Dry flies: Adams, Blue Dun, Blue-Winged Olive, Brown Hackle Peacock, Elkhair Caddis, Ginger Quill, Green Drake, Griffith Gnat, Humpy, Rio Grande King, Royal Wulff. Nymphs: Breadcrust, caddis emerger and larvae, Gold-Ribbed Hare's Ear, Green Drake Emerger, Halfback, Prince, Little Yellow Stone.

Basalt to Carbondale

In the town of Basalt the Fryingpan joins the Roaring Fork. Here the Fork becomes a major river. Even at low flows it's big. Although the gradient is lower here than it is above Basalt, the volume of water gives the current lots of strength.

➤ Access and Parking

State Highway 82 parallels the river between Carbondale and Basalt. County roads off 82 provide access to the Fork.

Basalt Three miles of river are open from the Lower Bypass Bridge just downstream from the confluence with Sopris Creek to the Upper Bypass Bridge east of town along State Highway 82.

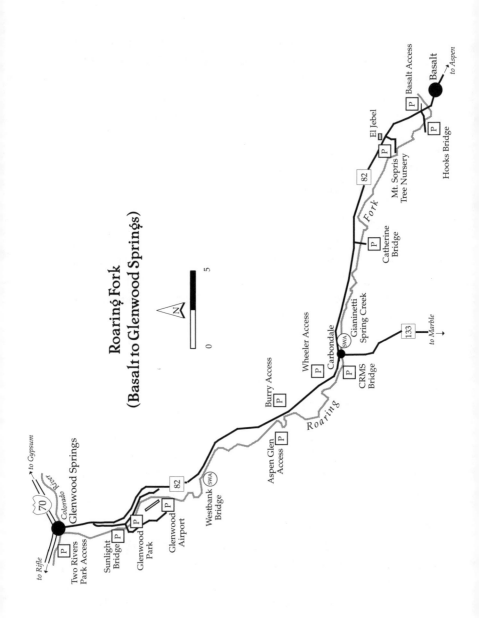

Roaring Fork
(Basalt to Glenwood Springs)

One and one-half miles east of El Jebel, Two Rivers Road (the old Highway 82) follows the right (north) bank of the Fork. You'll find several spots in which to park along the road on the shoulders.

Hooks Bridge A quarter-mile of the right (north) bank is open here. Take Willets Lane south (toward the river) after passing El Jebel, then right to the bridge.

El Jebel Go 7 miles east of Carbondale on State Highway 82 to the U.S. Forest Service tree nursery at El Jebel on Valley Road.

Catherine Bridge Catherine Bridge is south of State Highway 82 on County Road 100. Access is 30 feet from the centerline of the bridge on both sides.

Carbondale State Wildlife Area: Gianinetti Lease At Carbondale, State Highway 133 connects with Highway 82. On the southeast corner of the junction pull off the road into the parking area for marked access. The CDOW lease begins at the old bridge abutment and continues upstream about 2,015 feet to midstream from the Highway 82 side.

Gianinetti Spring Creek A half-mile of the Roaring Fork upstream of the Carbondale SWA, 2 miles of creek, and a small lake are open to angling for a fee. For information, contact: Gianinetti Ranch Spring Creeks, 601 Cowen Drive, Carbondale, CO 81623; (970) 963-0313.

➤ Seasons

This stretch is open for most of the year. It is a popular section with float fishermen before the runoff raises the water level too high. In the summer you will find good fly fishing here. The river can be floated again by late summer and fall. This section is often free of ice in winter due to the entry of warmer water from the Fryingpan.

➤ Equipment

The Fork's slippery rounded rocks make for hazardous wading unless you have felt soles or studs. The river is much larger

An angler hooks a fish on the Roaring Fork at the Gianinetti State Wildlife Area in Carbondale.

here, with deep holes, some of which are too deep to wade. Chest waders are essential.

↦ Patterns

Dry flies: Adams, Blue Dun, Blue-Winged Olive, Brown Hackle Peacock, Elkhair Caddis, Ginger Quill, Green Drake, Griffith Gnat, Humpy, Rio Grande King, Royal Wulff. Nymphs: Breadcrust, caddis emerger and larvae, Gold-Ribbed Hare's Ear, Green Drake Emerger, Halfback, Prince, Little Yellow Stone.

Carbondale to Glenwood Springs

This is the stretch most anglers think of when planning a trip to the Roaring Fork. If fishing from a raft, anglers have access to

11 miles of water. With the exception of the high-water season during runoff, wading fishermen can reach much of the river.

Some of the largest fish in the Fork are found on this stretch. One March day I watched Ray Sapp, a partner at The Colorado Angler in Lakewood, take not one but two rainbows of more than 20 inches. And we were still within the Glenwood Springs city limits.

❧ Access and Parking

State Highway 82 runs parallel to the Roaring Fork from Glenwood Springs to Carbondale. Between the traffic light by the railroad tracks on the south end of Glenwood and Buffalo Valley, the old highway gets you close to the river for about 3 miles.

CRMS Access Follow the Crystal River downstream from the CRMS bridge, which is west outside of Carbondale, to the confluence with the Fork. Fish upstream to Sutank Bridge on the south side of the Roaring Fork. This accesses a quarter-mile of the river.

Wheeler Access Exit State Highway 82 about 10 miles south of Glenwood. Follow the dirt road upstream to CDOW signs. You can fish a quarter-mile of the river here.

Burry Access At mile marker 9 south of Glenwood, 1 mile of river along the right (north) bank is open by permission.

Westbank State Wildlife Area At milepost 5 south of Glenwood on State Highway 82, turn right on Garfield County Road 154 to the river. About a quarter-mile of the river is open to public fishing. You may launch or take out a raft here.

Glenwood Airport About one-third of a mile of the river along the left (south) bank is open by the airport, which is city property. The airport is located south of the Sunlight Bridge along County Road 117, which goes to the Sunlight Ski Area.

Glenwood Park A half-mile of the river upstream of Three Mile Creek, as well as 200 feet extending downstream from it, is open along the left (south) side of the river. Access is from County Road 117.

Sunlight Bridge Near the south end of Glenwood, Old Highway 82 jogs off to the west toward the Roaring Fork. State Highway 117 heads toward Sunlight Ski Area at the Sunlight Bridge. Limited parking space is available near the bridge approaches, and steep paths lead down to the river. From here you can fish a half-mile upstream to Berthod Motors (county property) along the east bank and downstream for one-quarter mile.

Veltus Park This park is located on the west side of the river a couple hundred yards upstream from the confluence with the Colorado. This area has handicap access. City of Glenwood property gives access to the east side of the river between Seventeenth and Eighteenth Streets.

⌐ Seasons

Thanks to the low elevation around Glenwood Springs, the river comes alive in late February to mid-March. This just could be the best season to enjoy the Fork. The water is still cold but the warming trend awakens the fish from their winter lethargy. Insects come awake then, too. Hatches produce dry-fly action during the warm hours of midday. *Baetis* become active after noon when conditions are right. At 300 to 400 cfs, the river is easy to wade. In some sections anglers will be able to cross with little difficulty.

The Roaring Fork is not only a great stonefly river but it produces an incredible caddis hatch, the kind you read about but seldom experience. The rafter hatch begins in spring, too. That's not all bad, though, because floating the river is the only way to fish many of the private sections.

In early May, the river is usually fishable, but melting snows send a raging torrent down its channel later in the month. It's called the Roaring Fork for good reason. With flows that run as high as 6,000 cfs, forget about fishing. In spite of the large flows, big stoneflies hatch in June and offer good fishing in places you can reach.

The Fork is again easy to wade by midsummer. In the post-runoff period the river begins to drop and presents the angler with some of the state's finest dry-fly fishing. Mayfly and caddis hatches occur throughout the summer, though the caddis are not as prolific as in April. Smaller stoneflies hatch, too.

Fall puts the browns into a spawning mode. Mayflies and caddis still hatch through the fall, but their numbers decline as winter approaches. Flows are steady, having reached their low for the year. This is one of the best times to fish not only the Fork, but all of our Colorado rivers. By September anglers seem to have forgotten that the fish are still hitting. That means the streams are less crowded.

The Fork is a rarity. It's Colorado's only major free-flowing river that is fishable throughout the year. In spite of winter's efforts, the lower river downstream from Carbondale is usually open, though time on-stream will be limited. Slush ice is the problem. During this season, warm days present the best opportunity for wetting a line. Even then, it can be almost noon before the ice clears enough to allow fishing.

Whitefish are common on the Fork and will eagerly take a fly. In December this may be the most frequently taken fish. I have even caught a few on #4 stonefly nymphs.

➤ Equipment

The average size of the Fork's trout, its strong currents, and the slippery bottom make a rod of at least a 4-weight advisable. Cleats or studs on your boots will help provide better footing. For late-summer conditions—low, warmer flows—lightweight chest waders will be comfortable.

➤ Patterns

Dry flies: Adams, Blue Dun, Blue-Winged Olive, Brown Hackle Peacock, Elkhair Caddis, Ginger Quill, Green Drake, Griffith Gnat, Humpy, Rio Grande King, Royal Wulff. Nymphs: Breadcrust, caddis emerger and larvae, Gold-Ribbed Hare's Ear, Green Drake Emerger, Halfback, Prince, Little Yellow Stone. Streamers: Woolly Bugger, Spruce Fly, Muddler Minnow.

Roaring Fork Hatch Chart

	Jan	Feb	Mar	Apr	May	Jun	Jul	Aug	Sep	Oct	Nov	Dec
Blue-Winged Olive			▬	▬	▬				▬	▬	▬	
Green Drake						▬	▬	▬				
Pale Morning Dun						▬	▬	▬				
Caddis				▬	▬	▬	▬	▬				
Stoneflies												
Pteronarcys					▬							
Golden						▬	▬	▬				
Midges	▬	▬	▬	▬							▬	▬
Terrestrials							▬	▬	▬			

THE FRYINGPAN RIVER

The Fryingpan follows the course of a young canyon carved into the resistant red sandstone below Ruedi Reservoir. The Seven Castles, on the lower third of the river, form a prominent landmark.

Some of the finest fall fishing is available on the Pan. Even on cold days the few hours around noon provide dry-fly fishing with a few *Baetis* on the water.

At Basalt the Fryingpan joins the Roaring Fork. Between Basalt and Ruedi Dam the Pan offers about 15 miles of water. More than half of this length is private and inaccessible to anglers without permission. Some of the fly shops in the area have arrangements with landowners, who will allow access to anglers with a guide. The section below Ruedi Dam is classified as Gold Medal Water. In past years, the 4 miles below Ruedi Dam were designated catch-and-release. Currently it's catch-and-release for rainbows with a two-fish limit on browns under 14 inches.

A few years ago the big attraction was the rainbows below Ruedi that gorged themselves on mysis shrimp. Then the mysis and the rainbows declined for a while. Recently the mysis have returned to Ruedi, and they are eagerly taken by fish below the dam. The big rainbows are coming back.

The Fryingpan is small as rivers go. A tailwater fishery, the Pan's water is usually clear and wadable. Normal flows run around 100 cfs, with peak runoff flows approaching 1,000 cfs. Also because it is a tailwater fishery, part of the river is open through the winter. Wading the river except during runoff is accomplished with little difficulty—the bottom is good and solid.

135

Fryingpan River
(Ruedi Dam to Basalt)

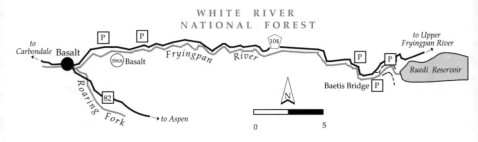

Felt-soled wading boots will handle most situations. Even with the river's high gradient you'll find many places to cross. A few holes, though, are quite deep. The upper few miles below Ruedi Dam run cold year-round. Water temperatures may be in the forties and low fifties.

Although most anglers concentrate on the tailwater—the mile of river immediately below the dam—don't pass up the lower runs merely to join the crowds. Summer angling can be as good there and is certainly less busy.

⌐ Access and Parking

At Glenwood Springs take State Highway 82 south, toward Basalt. The Fryingpan joins the Roaring Fork at Basalt 24 miles south of Glenwood Springs. Eagle County Road 104, known as the Fryingpan Road, follows the river upstream to Ruedi Reservoir. Access is available to the public on the Basalt State Wildlife

Area above Basalt and within the White River National Forest. The majority of the private land along the river is well marked, so there is no reason to get caught trespassing. Several parking areas in the state wildlife area and in the national forest provide plenty of access to the river where it's open.

White River National Forest Above the Basalt State Wildlife Area, the Fryingpan Road goes through alternating private and national forest land. Within the White River National Forest parking is available on the road shoulder. A mile downstream from the dam dirt roads provide access to the tailwater along both sides of the river.

Basalt State Wildlife Area The wildlife area begins just east of Basalt and continues upstream for about 3 miles. There is a single quarter-mile stretch of private land in this section where river access is not permitted. Parking in the wildlife area is in the one parking lot on the south side of the road, or along the road shoulder. Public access is marked by CDOW signposts.

➤ Seasons

By April most of the Fryingpan is open, even in the lower runs. Midge emergers are a good bet then in the tailwater. Mayflies begin showing up on the Pan in May and June.

As a tailwater fishery, the Pan is less affected by the spring runoff than are other area streams. The river's channel is small, though, and it doesn't take a large volume of water to make wading difficult. Flows exceeding 250 cfs require anglers to use caution.

When fly fishermen think of the Fryingpan, they think of green drakes, those gigantic mayflies the fish gorge on in midsummer. By mid-July running into September the Fryingpan is busy with the green drake hatch. The river is usually at its best: Flows are low, so the river is easy to wade; the water is clear, making it easy to locate fish. During the drake hatch the river is also busy with anglers. You may have to wait a while to get to fish the choice holes.

The Fryingpan River is open all year for a few miles below Ruedi Dam.

Fall puts the browns into a spawning mode. Mayfly and caddis still hatch through the fall, but their numbers decline as winter approaches. As with other rivers, the Pan is less crowded in September. The trout aren't the only reason to come here. Fall colors are especially attractive, contrasting with the reds of the canyon and deep blue sky.

The Fryingpan is ice-free for 2 or 3 miles through the winter, providing good nymph fishing then. On the warmer days and during the brief period when the sun reaches the river a *Baetis* hatch may occur, providing some fast action for a while on dry flies.

⚓ Equipment

The Fryingpan is a great river for a light rod. Downstream from the dam the fish average 10 to 14 inches; these are trout that can be played on a 2- or 3-weight. Since the currents can be strong, though, don't go overboard on the lightweights in order to avoid stressing the fish excessively. Any rod that will permit you to quickly play and release trout is fine. In the Toilet Bowl, the tailwater pool below the gate, a heavier rod is justified. The hogs, fed on mysis, are returning to the Pan. A 4-weight should still handle most fish caught here, and a 5- to 6-weight is also a good choice.

Ruedi is a bottom-release dam. The river runs cold through the year. Water temperatures in summer can be lower than 50 degrees. The Pan also has a number of deep holes that are not manageable with hip waders. Because of the deep holes and cold temperatures, chest-high neoprene waders are recommended.

➤ Patterns

Beginning in mid-July and running into September, the Fryingpan is busy with the green drake hatch. This is the insect the Pan is best known for. These are large mayflies, imitated with patterns in sizes #12–#16. The drakes usually begin hatching by midmorning to around noon. Activity lasts through most of the afternoon on good days. Before the drakes are on the water anglers should be able to catch fish on Green Drake emerger patterns. Be prepared to change flies quickly, because when the duns emerge, the fish forget about the nymphal form.

Although the green drake is the big attraction in summer, don't overlook other hatches. Pale morning duns and caddis also emerge at the same time. Terrestrials—ants, grasshoppers, and beetles—are around then, too.

Mysis shrimp are in the river year-round. Midges are too, but they interest the trout primarily in the winter months, when there are fewer insects hatching.

Dry flies: Adams, Blue Dun, Blue-Winged Olive, Elkhair Caddis, Green Drake, Griffith Gnat, Humpy (tied to imitate green drake dun), hoppers, ants, beetles. Nymphs: Caddis emerger and larvae, Gold-Ribbed Hare's Ear, Pheasant Tail, green drake emerger, midge emerger and larvae, mysis shrimp, Breadcrust.

Try to visit the Fryingpan during the week if at all possible. The four-hour drive from Denver and other Colorado metro areas does little to discourage anglers from making the trip on weekends, even in late fall. Fortunately, many anglers are also football fans. The day of the Colorado-Nebraska game often finds the river nearly devoid of fishermen.

Glenwood Springs has long been famous for hot springs and vapor caves. Geothermal activity deep within the earth is the source of the hot springs. It's a remnant of ancient volcanism, evidence of which is still found along Interstate 70 near Dotsero. The Glenwood Springs Hot Springs Pool and Vapor Caves are open year-round.

Fryingpan River Hatch Chart												
	Jan	Feb	Mar	Apr	May	Jun	Jul	Aug	Sep	Oct	Nov	Dec
Blue-Winged Olive			▓	▓	▓				▓	▓	▓	
Green Drake						▓	▓	▓				
Pale Morning Dun					▓	▓	▓					
Caddis					▓	▓	▓	▓				
Midges	▓	▓	▓	▓							▓	▓
Mysis Shrimp	▓	▓	▓	▓	▓	▓	▓	▓	▓	▓	▓	▓

FLY PATTERNS FOR THE COLORADO RIVER

> . . . and a broad-brimmed felt hat, the band of which was stuck full of flies of all sizes and a multitude of colors.
> —L. B. France, *Rod and Line in Colorado Waters*

No river guide is complete unless the author recommends a few fly patterns and gives directions for tying them. Since new patterns are continually emerging—much as the insects themselves the patterns are designed to imitate—any listing is necessarily incomplete. To complicate matters further, we may share a few favorite imitations in common, but the way I tie them will be different from how readers will tie them. Fortunately, the fish aren't usually picky. They seldom notice small variations in tail length, wing height, or other discrepancies. So for what it's worth, and to fulfill my obligation as a sage, here are some of my favorites.

Before going into the specifics of tying these patterns, we need to consider a few variables. Back in the 1970s, fly tiers had two choices in hooks: Mustad and the other maker, Mustad. Now, a new hook manufacturer goes into business every other week, so tiers have myriad brand names to select from. Because each tier will have certain favorite hooks, in the following patterns hooks will be listed by style rather than by specific make and model.

Patterns vary over time, too. A few years ago the preferred *Baetis* imitations were the Blue Quill and Blue Dun. The current standard is the Blue-Winged Olive, or BWO. Because patterns evolve, a new tie will be favored a few years from now and the BWO will be listed as an oldie but goodie.

Materials also change, as do tying methods. The modern version of the San Juan Worm is tied either with Ultra Chenille or some variation of tubular plastic extruded to an assortment of diameters. The original San Juan Worm used red wool for the body. Among the patterns mentioned in *The Treatise of Fishing with an Angle* is one named the Ruddy Fly. The work is attributed to Dame Juliana Berners, a mysterious fifteenth-century figure whose existence has never been proven. Yes, she did put wings on the Ruddy Fly, but otherwise it greatly resembles some modern ties for the Worm.

As good as synthetic materials are, nothing so far has come along to replace animal fur and hair. Development of dyeing technology gives us deer and elk hair in a rainbow assortment of colors while retaining the hair's natural qualities of buoyancy and durability. Dyed hair lets the tier vary the colors of standard patterns, such as the Humpy, for use as hatch-matching imitations.

Remember also that there is no one correct method of tying any pattern. Ask a dozen tiers to demonstrate the "standard" Gold-Ribbed Hare's Ear and you will be shown a dozen variations. All of them work, though, and that's what matters. Fish lack the ability to discriminate between the infinite assortment of fur and fluff we throw at them. It is doubtful if anyone knows just why a trout takes an artificial fly. All we really know is that they do take our offerings, sometimes. If they do, we can't ask much more of a pattern.

Although the recipes for some dry flies here specify hackle fibers for the tail, try a little improvement. The rivers in this guide tend to be boisterous in many sections. To help a fly float a little better in rough water, instead of hackle fibers tie it with a few strands of moose mane. The material is stiff enough to keep the largest pattern on top of the water.

A nice stonefly assortment for the Colorado River. From left: *Sofa Pillow, Yellow Stone, Halfback, Pat Dorsey's Paper Stone.*

On the same subject, try this for patterns calling for hair bodies. For Humpys and Elkhair Caddises in the larger sizes, #12–#16, substitute a wet-fly hook for a light-wire dry-fly model. This results in a little stronger fly that is less likely to straighten out in the jaws of a heavy fish. The hair makes the fly so buoyant that the heavier hook will still float like a cork.

As with any list of patterns, this one is necessarily incomplete. It is an assortment of imitations I have found to work on the Colorado. Unless otherwise noted, all recipes are from Randy Smith, a commercial tier.

Dry Flies

Pale Morning Dun

Hook:	Fine-wire dry fly
Size:	12–16
Tail:	Light dun or ginger hackle fibers
Body:	Pale yellow dubbing
Wing:	Light dun hen hackle tips
Hackle:	Ginger
Thread:	Dun 8/0

Blue-Winged Olive

Hook:	Fine-wire dry fly
Size:	16–24
Tail:	Dun hackle fibers
Body:	Olive dun dubbing
Wing:	Light gray hen hackle tips
Hackle:	Light dun
Thread:	Gray 8/0

Red Quill

Hook:	Fine-wire dry fly
Size:	14–18
Tail:	Medium-bronze dun hackle fibers
Body:	Brown rooster quill stem
Wing:	Lemon wood-duck flank fibers
Hackle:	Medium-bronze dun
Thread:	Gray 8/0

Royal Wulff
Hook: Fine-wire dry fly
Size: 14–18
Tail: Moose mane
Body: Peacock herl with red floss in center
Wing: White calf tail
Hackle: Coachman brown
Thread: Brown 8/0

Adams Irresistible
Hook: Fine-wire dry fly
Size: 14–18
Tail: Moose mane
Body: Spun deer hair, trimmed
Wing: Grizzly hackle tips
Hackle: Grizzly and brown
Thread: Brown 8/0

Elkhair Caddis
Hook: Wet fly similar to Mustad 3906B
Size: 12–18
Body: Hare's mask dubbing
Wing: Light or dark elk hair
Hackle: Brown
Thread: Tan 8/0

Goddard Caddis
Hook: Wet fly similar to Mustad 3906B
Size: 8–14
Body: Spun deer hair, trimmed to taper toward eye
Hackle: Brown
Thread: Tan 8/0
Antennae: Brown hackle stems

Humpy

Hook:	Wet fly similar to Mustad 3906B
Size:	12–18
Tail:	Deer hair
Body:	Deer hair
Underbody:	Red, yellow, olive, or black floss
Wing:	Deer hair
Hackle:	Brown
Thread:	Brown

Jack Dennis–Style Humpy

Hook:	Wet fly similar to Mustad 3906B
Size:	12–18
Tail:	Moose mane
Body:	Soft deer or elk hair, dyed to match the insect
Underbody:	Peacock herl
Wing:	Soft deer or elk hair, same color as body
Hackle:	Brown, grizzly, or dun, to match the insect
Thread:	Brown, use 3/0 Monocord for the larger sizes

Jack Dennis–Style Royal Humpy

Hook:	Wet fly similar to Mustad 3906B
Size:	12–18
Tail:	Moose mane
Body:	Soft deer or elk hair, light brown
Underbody:	Peacock herl
Wing:	White calf hair
Hackle:	Brown
Thread:	Brown, use 3/0 Monocord for the larger sizes

Sofa Pillow
Hook: 4X streamer
Size: 2–10
Tail: Red turkey quill
Body: Orange yarn
Rib: Brown hackle, fibers trimmed to stem
Wing: Elk hair tied Elkhair Caddis–style
Hackle: Brown, very densely tied
Thread: Brown
Antennae: Brown hackle stems

Nymphs

Halfback
Hook: 2XL
Size: 4–12
Tail: Pheasant-tail fibers
Abdomen: Peacock herl wrapped with brown hackle, overlay
            with pheasant-tail fibers as a wingcase
Thorax: Peacock herl, wrapped with brown hackle
Thread: Brown 3/0 Monocord

Twenty-Incher
Hook: 2XL
Size: 4–12
Tail: Brown goose biots
Abdomen: Peacock herl, ribbed with gold tinsel
Thorax: Tan dubbing
Legs: Mottled teal or mallard flank feathers
Wingcase: Mottled turkey quill
Thread: Brown 3/0 Monocord

Pat Dorsey's Paper Stone

Hook:	4XL streamer
Size:	4–12
Tail:	Brown goose biots
Abdomen:	Brown or black dubbing. Tyvec wound over dubbing
Thorax:	Brown or black dubbing
Wingcase:	Tyvec
Legs:	Pheasant-tail fibers
Thread:	Brown or black 6/0
Antennae:	Brown goose biots

Prince

Hook:	Heavy-wire wet fly, 2X
Size:	8–16
Tail:	Brown goose biots
Body:	Peacock herl, ribbed with gold tinsel
Wing:	White goose biots
Hackle:	Soft brown
Thread:	Black

Gold-Ribbed Hare's Ear

Hook:	Heavy-wire wet fly, 2X
Size:	8–18
Tail:	Hare's mask
Abdomen:	Hare's mask (cheek) dubbing, ribbed with gold tinsel
Thorax:	Hare's mask (cheek) dubbing
Wingcase:	Brown turkey quill
Thread:	Brown 6/0

Pheasant Tail

Hook:	Heavy-wire wet fly, 2X
Size:	12–18
Tail, abdomen:	Pheasant-tail fibers
Thorax:	Peacock herl
Wingcase:	Pheasant-tail fibers
Legs:	Pheasant-tail fibers
Thread:	Brown 8/0

Randy's Scud

Hook:	Scud or wide-gap
Size:	10–16
Tail:	Hackle fibers to match body color
Body:	Olive, tan, or orange Ligas dubbing
Back:	Strip of plastic freezer bag
Rib:	4-pound monofilament
Thread:	Same as body color, 6/0

San Juan Worm

Hook:	Scud or wide-gap
Size:	12–16
Body:	Tubular colored-plastic lace with a strand of sparkle material inside, wound on hook. Alternate method: Strip of Ultra Chenille tied to hook at center

Midges

Black Zing Wing Pupa

Hook:	Dai-Riki 310
Size:	20–26
Body:	6/0 black thread
Wing:	Zing Wing or Krystal Flash
Thread:	Black 8/0

Black Beauty

Hook:	Dai-Riki 305
Size:	20–26
Body:	6/0 black thread
Rib:	Copper wire
Thorax:	Black dubbing
Thread:	Black 8/0

Black Biot Midge Pupa

Hook:	Dai-Riki 135
Size:	20–22
Body:	Black goose biot
Thorax:	Black dubbing
Thread:	Black 8/0

Brassie

Hook:	Dai-Riki 135
Size:	18–22
Body:	Fine copper wire
Thorax:	Black dubbing
Thread:	Black 8/0

Emergers

Gold-Ribbed Hare's Ear
Hook: Heavy-wire wet fly, 2X
Size: 16–22
Tail: Pheasant-tail fibers
Abdomen: Olive dubbing, ribbed with fine gold wire
Thorax: Olive dubbing
Wingcase: Krystal Flash or pearl Flashabou
Thread: Olive 8/0

RS-2
Hook: Wet fly
Size: 18–22
Tail: 2 moose-mane fibers
Body: Gray dubbing
Wing: White marabou
Thread: Gray 8/0

Serendipity
Hook: Wet fly or scud
Size: 18–22
Body: Polypropylene yarn in gray, brown, yellow, or tan
Wing: Trimmed deer hair with Krystal Flash
Thread: 6/0, same color as body

APPENDIX

WaterTalk

The Colorado Division of Water Resources operates a monitoring system of the state's rivers. By satellite telemetry, water flows from gauges throughout the state are reported to a computer at Water Resources. This information is updated every four hours at most locations. To access the system you need only a touch-tone telephone. Once you are connected to the system, you will be instructed by the computer what to do next.

The state is divided into seven districts, each covering a major drainage system. When calling WaterTalk, you will be instructed to select the division, then the station. The Colorado River and its tributaries are in Division 5. After calling WaterTalk at (303) 831-7135, at the voice prompt enter 5, followed by an asterisk (*), then give the station number followed by another asterisk (*). When you are finished, press the pound (#) to disconnect, then hang up.

The following division and station numbers are of interest to anglers. For a complete listing of WaterTalk stations, contact: Office of the State Engineer, Division of Water Resources, 1313 Sherman Street, Room 818, Denver, CO 80203; (303) 866-3581.

River	Division	Station
Blue, below Dillon Reservoir	5	1
Blue, below Green Mountain Reservoir	5	2

River	Division	Station
Colorado, near Dotsero	5	4
Colorado, below Granby Reservoir	5	5
Colorado, below Glenwood Springs	5	6
Colorado, near Kremmling	5	7
Colorado, near Granby	5	8
Colorado, near Hot Sulphur Springs	service discontinued*	
Eagle, below Gypsum	5	14
Eagle, at Red Cliff	5	15
Fraser, near Windy Gap	5	16
Fryingpan, near Ruedi	5	17
Roaring Fork, near Aspen	5	30
Roaring Fork, below Maroon Creek	5	31
Roaring Fork, at Glenwood Springs	5	32
Williams Fork, below Williams Fork Reservoir	5	41

*To calculate the approximate flow at Hot Sulphur Springs, subtract the Williams Fork flow from that of the Colorado River near Kremmling.

You may also get this information from TravelBank Systems with a computer and modem. System operator Jay Melnick updates the flows frequently. In addition to water flows, TravelBank Systems carries outdoor activity information for skiers, hikers, bikers, and photographers as well as for anglers and hunters. To access TravelBank Systems via your computer modem, dial (303) 671-7669. Setup is No Parity, 8 Data Bits, 1 Stop Bit, speed to 14,400 bps. Follow the online prompts. The best time to call this number is in the evenings. There is no fee other than the phone call for using this service. For a modest annual fee you may subscribe to the multi-line service, on which you'll experience fewer busy signals. You'll see this information online.

Fly Shops and Lodges

These shops will provide information, and most can arrange guided fishing on the Colorado or tributary streams.

Denver Area

Anglers All
5211 South Santa Fe
Littleton, CO 80120
(303) 794-1104

Blue Quill Angler
Mark Harrington, Jim Cannon
1532 Evergreen Parkway
Evergreen, CO 80439
(303) 674-4700

Colorado Angler
Ray and Rhonda Sapp
1457 Nelson Street
Lakewood, CO 80215
(303) 232-8298

The Complete Angler
Bill Grems
8547 East Arapahoe Road
Englewood, CO
(303) 694-2387

The Fly Fisher Ltd.
252 Clayton Street
Denver, CO 80206
(303) 322-5014

The Trout Fisher Incorporated
Len Sanders
2020 South Parker Road
Aurora, CO 80231
(303) 369-7970

Middle Park Area

Buggywhip's
Jim Blackburn
Post Office Box 770479
Steamboat Springs, CO 80477
(970) 879-8033

Fishin' Hole Sporting Goods
Bill Janson
309 Park Avenue, Box 435
Kremmling, CO 80459
(970) 724-9407

Fletcher's Sporting Goods
Jim and Georgia Kauffman
217 West Agate Avenue
 (U.S. 40)
Granby, CO 80446
(970) 887-3747

Mountain Angler, Ltd.
311 South Main Street
Breckenridge, CO 80424
(970) 453-4665

Nelson Fly & Tackle Shop
Jim and Kathy Nelson
72149 Highway 40, Box 336
Tabernash, CO 80478
(303) 726-8558

Riverside Anglers
Riverside Hotel
Hot Sulphur Springs, CO 80451
(970) 725-0025

Glenwood Springs Area—Lower Colorado River

Colorado Division of Wildlife
50633 Highway 6 and 24
Glenwood Springs, CO 81601
(970) 945-7228

Fly Fishing Outfitters
Bill Perry, Pat Moore
Post Office Box 2861
Avon, CO 81620
(970) 476-3474

Roaring Fork Anglers
Tim Heng
2022 Grand Avenue
Glenwood Springs, CO 81601
(970) 945-0180

Basalt-Aspen Area: Roaring Fork and Fryingpan Rivers

Alpine Angling
48 Weant Boulevard
Carbondale, CO 81623
(970) 963-9245

Aspen Outfitting at
  Aspen Sports
303 East Durant Avenue
Ritz-Carlton Hotel
Aspen, CO 81611
(970) 925-6332 or
  (970) 925-3406

Frying Pan Anglers
123 Emma Road
River Park Center, Unit 100
Basalt, CO 81621
(970) 927-3441

Oxbow Outfitting
623 East Durant Avenue
Little Nell Hotel
Aspen, CO 81611
(970) 925-1505 or
  (800) 421-1505

Pomeroy Sports/Aspen
  Trout Guides
614 East Durant Avenue
Aspen, CO 81611
(970) 925-7875 or
  (970) 920-1050

Snowmass Oxbow Outfitters
Snowmass Village Mall
Post Office Box 6068
Snowmass Village, CO 81615
(970) 923-5959 or
  (800) 247-2755

Western Sports
19400 Highway 82, Unit D
Carbondale, CO 81623
(970) 963-3030
(Next to City Market at El Jebel)

Access to Private Water

Elktrout Lodge
1853 County Road 33
Post Office Box 614
Kremmling, CO 80459
(303) 724-3343

Gianinetti Ranch Spring Creeks

601 Cowen Drive
Carbondale, CO 81623
(970) 963-0313
Private access on the Roaring
Fork, spring creeks, and lake.

Hurd Creek Ranch & Fishing
  Club
P.O. Box 516
Tabernash, CO 80478
(970) 726-5304

Rocky Mountain Angling Club
6099 South Quebec, Suite 102
Englewood, CO 80111
(303) 793-1993 or
  (800) 524-1814
Fax: (303) 793-0549
Access for members on private
water on the Colorado and
other rivers.

The International Whitewater Scale: Classification of Rapids

For those who plan to float navigable sections of the Colorado, Eagle, and Roaring Fork Rivers, the following distinguishes water types. This scale is included in the BLM publication, *Upper Colorado River Recreation Area.*

Class I: Very easy. Moving water with a few riffles and small waves. Few or no obstructions.

Class II: Easy. Easy rapids with waves to three feet and wide clear channels visible without scouting. Some maneuvering required.

Class III: Medium difficulty. Rapids with high irregular waves capable of swamping an open canoe. Narrow passages often requiring complex maneuvering and scouting from shore.

Class IV: Difficult. Long difficult rapids with constricted passages often requiring precise maneuvering in very turbulent waters. Scouting from shore is often necessary, and conditions make rescue difficult. Not runnable in open canoes.

Class V: Very difficult. Long and violent rapids with highly congested routes nearly always requiring scouting from shore. Rescue conditions are difficult. Significant hazards to life in event of mishap. Ability to Eskimo-roll kayaks is essential.

Class VI: Extremely dangerous. Nearly impossible to run and very dangerous. For teams of experts only after close study, having taken all precautions.

Colorado Division of Wildlife. *Colorado Fishing Season Information and Wildlife Property Directory.* Denver, CO: Colorado Division of Wildlife, December 1995.

Colorado Division of Wildlife. *Colorado Gold Medal Waters.* Denver, CO: Colorado Division of Wildlife, 1993.

Colorado Division of Wildlife. *Supplement to the Colorado Wildlife Property Directory: State Trust Lands.* Denver, CO: Colorado Division of Wildlife, June 1996.

Corle, Greg. "Colorado's I-70 Trout." *Rocky Mountain Game & Fish,* Vol. 1995, No. 4, Game & Fish Publications. April 1995: page 20.

Fishing Map and Guide, Fryingpan and Roaring Fork Rivers. Basalt, CO: Edited and published by Rivers Publishing, Inc., 1995.

France, L. B. *With Rod and Line in Colorado Waters.* 1884. Reprint, Boulder, CO: Pruett Publishing Company, 1996.

Kelly, Tim. *Tim Kelly's Fishing Guide, 17th Edition.* Edited by Donald Hart, Denver, CO: Hart Publications, 1985.

Powell, John Wesley. *The Exploration of the Colorado River and its Canyons.* 1895. Reprint, New York: Dover, 1961.

U.S. Bureau of Land Management. *The Upper Colorado River Recreation Area.* Washington, DC: U.S. Government Printing Office, 1991.

INDEX

With over thirty years of fly fishing experience in Colorado, Al Marlowe also teaches fly fishing and ties his own flies when time permits. He is a contributor to magazines such as *Colorado Outdoors* and *Rocky Mountain Game & Fish,* and is the author of *A Guide to the Flat Tops Wilderness.* Most importantly, Al enjoys fly fishing along the Colorado River with his wife Jean and dog Skipper—a respectable angler in his own right.